An Ordinary Bloke

Eugene Veith, the making
of a modern mystic

I met Eugene Veith, or 'Curly' as I came to know him, when I was confronted by a man in a hat who stuttered. He wanted to secure the contract for the Chef factory transport. We agreed to a trial then and it soon turned into a full scale trucking business for Chef which lasted for over thirty years. I quickly learned that Eugene was not only a supplier of a first class reliable service, but a very humble God-fearing man whose extraordinary generosity and care for those who were disadvantaged and for the Kingdom of God, was remarkable. His philanthropic involvements were extensive - world-wide in fact - and over the years we together investigated various proposals for investment and/or assistance. Eugene was not only a humble very real Christian, who lived frugally himself, but he used his substance for others. His is an inspirational story and his influence through the charitable entity he set up, 'Entrust,' continues on today very successfully. Of Eugene it could rightly be said: "He being dead yet speaketh." Hebrews 11:4

Harold Seeley AM,
Former CEO Chef Company

This is an extraordinary Australian story of an "ordinary bloke" gathered together by Jill Manton who, at his invitation, listened this remarkable man's soul into expression. Skilfully crafted, carefully framed, theologically nuanced, it is told with affection and respect. The result is a testament to the gift that is created when one listens with depth and compassion to another's story.

The book is richly layered. It quickly engages the general reader. For those in the helping professions, it invites you to witness the power of deeply compassionate listening to one human being by a trusted other. For those interested in preserving the wealth of stories the elders of our clans hold which call for telling, it is an invitation to act; to gather the harvest. For readers interested in the life of the Spirit, it is a story of one human being's spiritual formation and deep transformation as he sought to reflect the heart of his God in the "nitty gritty" of daily life. His success left an enduring legacy of abundant giving which enriched the lives of countless individuals and keeps on giving. An easily accessible, evocative account, this book enlarges the sensibility of the reader; a rare gift.

Diana Kelly-Byrne,
Ph.D. Consultant psychologist, writer and educator, Melbourne

Many of our immediate thoughts when talking about leading businessmen vacillate around 'driven', 'hard-nosed', 'exploitative', 'self-centred' and similar terms. That a very different kind of businessman can exist is the subject of this beautifully written reflective biography by Melbournian Jill Manton, well known for her leadership in spiritual formation. In the pages of this book we are privileged to meet Eugene Veith, whose outer success is more than matched by his inner spiritual life. In fact, we are stunned by the discovery that a prominent businessman can be a modern Christian mystic, whose inner world produced so much goodness, compassion and justice in our world and continues to do so today some years after his death.

Charles Ringma,
Professor Emeritus of Regent College, Canada, theologian, activist, author of *Hear the Ancient Wisdom* and many other books on Christian spirituality.

This book offers you the chance to get a glimpse into the heart of one of God's unusual servants. He was born just over 100 years ago - a humble, ordinary bloke whose love for God led him to establish a business that distributed all its profits to diverse forms of Christian mission in Australia and overseas. He had a special concern for children, abused women and the poor. Before his death the Entrust Foundation was established to ensure that this work would continue beyond his lifetime. Today it continues to grow, touching the lives of thousands of people in 15 nations. Jill Manton knew Eugene well and has beautifully captured his thinking, motivation, humanity and generosity. Her book will inspire and challenge you to do all you can with what you have - just as Eugene did!

Richard Beaumont,
CEO *Entrust Foundation*

Profits from the sale of this book will go to the Entrust Foundation

To the memory of my grandparents
Ralph and Mabel Garrett

An Ordinary Bloke
Eugene Veith, the making
of a modern mystic

JILL L. MANTON

a. Acorn Press

Published by Acorn Press
An imprint of Bible Society Australia
ACN 148 058 306 | Charity licence 19 000 528
GPO Box 4161
Sydney NSW 2001
Australia
www.acornpress.net.au | www.biblesociety.org.au

ISBN 978-0-647-53355-0

First published by Morning Star Publishing in 2016, ISBN 978-0-994-47078-2

Jill L. Manton asserts her right under section 193 of the *Copyright Act 1968* (Cth)
to be identified as the author of this work.

Where indicated, Scripture quotations are from the *New Revised Standard Version
Bible,* copyright © 1989 the Division of Christian Education of the National
Council of Churches of Christ in the United States of America.
Used by permission. All rights reserved.

Where indicated, Scripture quotations marked KJV are taken from the King
James Version, public domain.

A catalogue record for this
work is available from the
NATIONAL
LIBRARY   National Library of Australia
OF AUSTRALIA

Cover and text design and layout by John Healy
Cover image courtesy of *The Age*, Angel Wylie/Fairfax Syndication

CONTENTS

Foreword

I grew up in Melbourne and during that time I saw many a Veith Transport vehicle on the roads and I heard about the man behind these familiar trucks. I quickly gathered that he was a well-known, well-respected Christian businessman who was a generous supporter of Christian missions and other Christian organisations. Later on, I met him in person and was impressed with his warmth and humility.

This story is a lovely chronicle of his life as he understood it, carefully gathered together by Jill Manton from his reflections with her. It is a moving and inspiring read. I felt as though I was sitting with Eugene listening to him as he opened up about the deep things in his life. It is a significant work, lovingly crafted, about a fine man.

Reading it takes one to the places of formation in his life: a poor but loving childhood in rural Gippsland; anxious days as a teenager in Melbourne coping with a constant stammer and early hair loss; and working from an early age in his father's butcher business. Threaded through the recollections is his constant reflection on God's gentle ways and call on his life – and his lifelong desire to 'mean business with the Lord.'

The outcome of this desire in Eugene's heart led to an exemplary life of outstanding business acumen and what he achieved with it – the generosity which flowed to many individual people and Christian causes and organisations in Australia and around the world. One of these, which I acknowledge with gratitude, was World Vision Australia which I currently lead. Another perhaps less well known expression of his desire to be doing the 'Lord's work' was the practice of humble healing prayer and pastoral care he extended tirelessly to so many who came across his path.

It is good to have this record of a life of principle and a heart for God as a gift to the coming generations. I heartily commend it to you.

Tim Costello
CEO World Vision Australia

Prologue

Mystics are quite ordinary people: shoemakers, nannies, dyers of wool, home-care workers, or physicists.

Dorothee Soelle, *The Silent Cry*[1]

The mysticism of everyday life is the deepest mysticism of all.

Jurgen Moltmann[2]

"Vale Curly, your generous heart lives on." Who was Curly? This is his story. Eugene Veith was born in the eastern suburbs of Melbourne, Australia, in September 1915 and died at the age of ninety-five in September 2010. From difficult beginnings, at a young age he established a delivery business that under his leadership became the largest capital city metro parcel organisation in Australia. Most of the profits from Eugene's business venture were used to support diverse Christian ministries in Australia and around the world. He had a particular passion for supporting ministries that proclaimed the Gospel in word and action by challenging unjust social structures, empowering people living in poverty to move into more just and prosperous lives, and supporting leaders in teaching and preaching. He left a continuing legacy through the Entrust Foundation, which he established in 2008, shortly before his death in 2010. But as well as his business, Eugene has left an enduring heritage in the lives of hundreds, probably thousands of people, whom he influenced in many life-giving ways.

Several of Eugene's colleagues and friends have recognised his remarkable story in "Just call me Curly," a DVD produced in 2004. In May 2010, the Melbourne *Age* ran a front-page article on his life: "A long life of giving by a bald 'no-hoper' called Curly has given hope to thousands."[3] When he died in September, the newspaper published another article: "Vale Curly, your generous heart lives on." These stories of Eugene's life focus on his many gifts and wide interests, as well as his generosity, integrity, humility and faith. They are glimpses into how others saw him.

But many years before these publications, when Eugene was in his early seventies, he surprised me by suggesting that I might listen to his story, and eventually write it. Friends had been pressuring him about a biography, but he was hesitant because he felt it was important that whatever was written should not be a standard biography, but rather the story of God in his life. He wanted it to reflect how this relationship was the driving force of all his living – marriage, family, business, church, society – and his place in the wider world.

When Eugene first approached me in 1989, I had known him for over twenty years. Although he was old enough to be my father, we were good friends who knew each other well. We had a warm respect and affection for each other, enjoying times of rich conversation and prayer. There were few people I admired as much because, more than most of us, he lived what he believed. I felt in tune with what he was asking, and so I agreed, albeit with some trepidation. At the time we could not envisage exactly what this book might look like. But it evolved into this homely story of his life and prayer, as told by him in his later years to a good friend, with the reader invited to listen in. It is the story of his life as he understood it, from the inside out.

We met together over several months to converse about his life. Our conversations were recorded on an old tape machine that rested on a chair beside us. We would forget all about it until an arresting click would signify that it was time to turn over the tape, or to insert a blank one so the recording could continue. The time together was relaxed and informal, and we enjoyed it.

In subsequent years, we often talked about the project, and Eugene always reaffirmed the approach we had chosen. Just a few months before his death in September 2010, we re-read the transcripts of the old audio tapes and reflected on them. He was more than twenty years older than when we had initially recorded our conversations, and we had now known each other for over forty years. There was a new frailty about him and his hearing was worse. He moved slowly, unless he was zipping around in his bright red scooter, which gave him the mobility and independence his ageing legs denied him. But still present were the laughter and tears, the deep love of God, the gentle strength, the graciousness—now widened, mellowed and confirmed with the experience of the intervening years.

With very few exceptions, he was happy for his reflections to appear in print. We did not attempt to add all that had happened in the years following our interviews, deciding that any important details could be included as an epilogue in the publication. It was not long after this that he passed over into the wide, beautiful love he had long anticipated.

My memories of Eugene during the months of our interviews are still vivid. Again and again, he told me, "I'm an ordinary bloke, just an ordinary bloke."[4] Outwardly, there was certainly nothing remarkable about him. Of medium height and build, he dressed neatly, but unobtrusively. Usually, he wore a conservative suit of some sort or a jacket with well-tailored trousers. He was the sort of person who might live at the end of my street or travel with me on the same tram to work each day.

But there was always the hat—a discreet nod to good style, worn with ease, even a little jauntily. Sometimes he left it behind after one of our meetings and would later return ruefully to claim it. Whenever he greeted a lady outside, he raised his hat in a courteous gesture, revealing an old-fashioned courtliness that was genuine and gracious and also suggested that he was not such an ordinary man after all.

If we passed in the street, I would not have stopped to get another look at him. And I probably would not have noticed him much at a party either—unless I happened to be standing beside him and he drew me into conversation. His interest was real, not superficial, and when he engaged in conversation, he stood with a slight stoop, his head tilted toward the speaker. A degree of deafness leant extra care to his listening and a slight hesitance of speech caused him to choose his words carefully.

When I knew him, his face was surprisingly smooth, though creased in places with the lines of age—mostly crinkled laughter lines around his eyes. Behind nondescript glasses, his grey eyes were kind and gentle, and laughter was never far away. He had an attractive warmth and humility, which graced his conversations with rare and endearing compassion and understanding. An ordinary bloke? Perhaps so. Perhaps not. Perhaps both ordinary and extraordinary at the same time.

Although Eugene had an avid desire for learning and read widely until his death, his chief interest was to grasp more clearly what it meant for him to live his faith in what he called "the nitty-gritty of life." This desire was present in all of his study, contemplation of Scripture, worship and prayer, however caught up into the glory, beauty and joy of God he may often have been. His deep longing was to incarnate this inward experience outward as he lived his everyday life. He was, as he said, a very "ordinary bloke," yet he was able to express in his ordinary life the depth and breadth of his love affair with God. In this sense he might be called a "vernacular theologian,"[5] a term sometimes applied to St Francis of Assisi, because he expressed the ecstasy of his communion with God in his daily relationships with all of nature and the people he met.

Under the external narrative of his story, I heard the sound of a lifetime immersed in Scripture— "the Word" as he so frequently referred to it. I began to notice his profound, yet commonsense, understanding of discernment and his insistence on the importance of balance in all things, including the life of faith. This was reflected in the steady integration he maintained between his inner and outer life—the former growing deeper as the latter grew wider. This correlation was the hallmark of his life.

Beneath all he said was the constant refrain of his love for God. His faithful commitment to growing in this mutual love between God and himself was as basic for him as breathing. This included obedience to what he had come to understand as the ways of God in both the small and large things. "Meaning business with the Lord" was his favourite way of putting it and this also involved his returning to God's way if for some reason, either intentionally or unintentionally, he had "stepped out of line with the Lord." He was remarkably practical in his life of repentance and forgiveness, as he was in all spheres of his life. He did not like to have anything unresolved between himself and God, or his wife and children. This attitude overflowed into all his relationships, and he was quick to apologise if he had been in the wrong, or if he felt he had unintentionally hurt someone. Through painful times, he learned the importance of forgiving himself and of accepting God's forgiveness and he encouraged others to do the same.

When he spoke movingly and reverently of his communion with God in contemplation and prayer, I was frequently reminded of the Christian mystical tradition. Of course, this observation would not have occurred to Eugene any more than it would have occurred to any of those we now always associate with that tradition. It is what others notice about them, rather than the way they would describe themselves.

As far as I am aware, Eugene was not conscious in any detail of the lives or writings of most Christian mystics, although he told me that he had been blessed by some writings of Madame Jeanne Guyon,[6] Brother Lawrence[7] and Archbishop Fenelon.[8] He was struck by a story he had heard about an English Lord who stayed with Fenelon and was so challenged by the

Archbishop's life that he left early, saying that if he stayed longer he would have to become a Christian.

In passing, Eugene mentioned that although he had read a few mystical writings, they didn't appeal to him as much as the "more straightforward theological stuff". As I worked on the material from our interviews, this comment seemed ironical, and yet it underscored for me that the language and deep emotion with which he expressed times of profound communion with God were coming from deep within his own experience and were not something lightly spoken from his reading or other outside sources. I recall too, that after hearing Eugene speak at a gathering for spiritual directors, a Roman Catholic priest commented to me that he felt Eugene had been to the seventh dwelling place in St. Teresa's *The Interior Castle*.[9]

During our conversations, Eugene was often moved to tears of sadness or compassion, gratitude or joy. There were also frequent moments of spontaneous laughter, even hilarity. He felt deeply the difficulty of describing his experience, and this was intensified by his stammer and shyness. The fact that he engaged with me in such an extended reflection on his life struck him as simultaneously humorous and miraculous.

He particularly struggled to express his experience of God, often lamenting the inadequacy of words to convey what he was trying to say. I was deeply moved by his hushed reverence when he spoke of God's loving presence, great beauty or generous goodness and of his times of deep communion. But it is impossible to capture fully in words the hidden depths within a person's soul, the illuminating revelations of God, or the quiet pervasive sensation of the divine presence. Perhaps poetry and music at their best come closest to evoking this. *The Oxford Book of Mystical Verse* alludes to this difficulty: "The speech of everyday has no terms for what they have seen and known, and least of all can they hope for adequate expression through the phrases and apparatus of logical reasoning."[10] Dorothy Soelle also attests to this problem in *The Silent Cry: Mysticism and Resistance*: "It is a basic experience that language is too small, too narrow, too dusty, too unexpressive and too misleading to give word to the mystic condition."[11]

As far as possible, I have sought to tell Eugene's story in his own words, with their distinctly Australian flavour. September 2015 marked one hundred years since his birth – a significant anniversary. Remembering this, we will appreciate why his language is not inclusive and may sometimes seem outdated, even jarring to our ears. It will help us if we can let such time-constrained matters go in order to enter into the timeless truths of his words. As we hear Eugene's story, we may also be surprised by how far ahead of his time he seemed to be. In keeping with these characteristics of his, when quoting Scripture I have chosen sometimes to use the King James Version as that which formed Eugene in his faith, and on other occasions the New Revised Standard Version as representative of more modern versions he came to know and appreciate, whichever seemed more appropriate.

When Eugene looks back on his life, he notices how the seeds sown in his childhood shaped his journey with God. He is surprised by the way that these fragile beginnings gradually grew into an expansive diversity he could not imagine in his early years. In drawing near to Eugene's story, we may discover points of resonance within our own lives. Where does his story touch ours or move us? Do the questions he asked himself and God invite us to explore our own? Might his perspectives open us to new insights and alert us to those in our families who are ageing, encouraging us to invite them to reflect on and share their stories?

In the narrative that follows, my hope is that those who knew Eugene, along with those who are meeting him for the first time in these pages, will have the intuitive feeling that he is not far away, that the veil between this life and the next is thin and that his story itself is a potential thin place for us.[12] Eugene saw his pilgrimage with and into God as the key to everything he became, and his honest account of that journey is both profound and ordinary. Mixed into that paradox, we may see reflected the unfolding story of an Australian mystic in the making.

Jill Manton
Somers 2016

Endnotes throughout the book provide wider historical, social, religious, business and family contexts to Eugene's story for readers who are interested. They also help to bridge the gap between Eugene's reflections in 1989 and his death in 2010, as does the Epilogue. For those who would like to know more about the continuing story of Eugene's life through the Entrust Foundation visit its website www.entrust.org.au.

Endnotes

1 Soelle, Dorothee. *The Silent Cry: Mysticism and Resistance.* . Minneapolis, MN: Fortress Press, 2001,18.

2 Cited in Macrina Wiederkehr, *Seven Sacred Pauses: Living Mindfully through the Day.* Notre Dame, Indiana, Sorin Books, 2008, 19.

3 The Age is a leading Melbourne newspaper. Eugene frequently described himself as a "bald no-hoper," whose life was healed and turned around by the grace of God. Hence the newspaper headline.

4 Bloke is an Australian colloquialism for a man.

5 Delio, Ilia OSF. *Franciscan Prayer.* Cincinnati, OH: St Anthony Messenger Press, 2004, 7.

6 Madame Jeanne Guyon (1648-1717), French mystic, leading figure in the Quietism movement, writer on the spiritual life.

7 Brother Lawrence (1614-1691), lay brother in a Carmelite monastery in Paris, author of *The Practice of the Presence of God.*

8 Francois Fenelon (1651-1715), French Roman Catholic archbishop, theologian, poet and writer.

9 St.Teresa of Avila wrote *The Interior Castle* in 1577 as a guide for the sisters of her Carmelite Order in the development of their faith, prayer and service. The seventh dwelling place was at the centre of the Castle, the place of union with God.

10 Nicholson, D. H. S. and Lee, A. H. E eds. *The Oxford Book of Mystical Verse.* 1917; reprint, Oxford: Clarendon Press, 1947, vi.

11 Soelle, Dorothee: *The Silent Cry: Mysticism and Resistance.* Translated by Barbara and Martin Rumscheidt. Minneapolis, MN: Fortress Press, 2001, 56.

12 Celtic term for places where the separation between this life and the wider dimension of life that enfolds us seems thin, or transparent.

I

From time to time [we need] to enter that still room within us all where the past lives on as a part of the present, where the dead are alive again, where we are most alive ourselves to turnings and to where our journeys have brought us. The name of the room is Remember—the room where with patience, with charity, with quietness of heart, we remember consciously to remember the lives we have lived.[1]

Frederick Buechner, *A Room Called Remember*

Entering a room called remember

Set up road markers for yourself, make yourself signposts; consider well the highway, the road by which you went.

Jeremiah 31:21 NRSV

I'm nothing special you know—just an ordinary bloke. When I look back over my life, I am amazed at how it has all turned out. Whenever friends have suggested that someone should write my biography, I've laughed it off and changed the subject, but it keeps on being raised, forcing me to consider. Perhaps there is something in it after all.

But what I have in mind is not what most people think about when they suggest a biography. You see, the way I understand the story of my life is that it is really a story about God. When I remember how it has been to awaken to God and the effects of that waking up as it has rippled through my years, I know this is the story that interests me and which I would like to tell. But I am no writer, so I have chosen someone who knows me well and understands where I am coming from to prompt me to tell my story and then gather together all my messy musings and make of them a story told in my voice.

Though I feel shy and awkward talking about myself, it is inviting to have the chance to reflect on my life in this way. I am surprised at the memories that have been flowing back so easily and vividly. I'm interested in them, because there must be hundreds of thousands of others which I have forgotten. What then is the significance of these? Why have I recalled them and not others? How have they shaped my life so far and how do they continue to form me—for good and ill? I am beginning to see patterns emerging and threads which appear and disappear and reappear again later. It's hard to see these patterns when you are living them at the time, but looking back, it's easier and very illuminating. I've already lived my threescore years and ten and more, so attending to these memories is giving me space to pause and look back over the way I've travelled—rather like stopping to get breath after climbing to the top of a fairly steep hill. I value the new perspective this gives me, and I know that if I procrastinate too long, the opportunity may not come again.

I am noticing how layered my memories are with deep feelings that I did not anticipate. My childhood and adolescent experiences are so clear and vivid! And as the intense feelings come surging back, I have the sense that I am seeing and feeling as both the child or youth I was and the man I have become in my seventh decade of life. The latter perspective provides me with a lens through which I can view my earlier life, prompting insights and questions that were impossible when I was younger, while also giving me far wider understanding and compassion of these present years.

In some ways, this is like riding a roller coaster, yet I'm gradually becoming aware of the flow of my life as I go deeper into my awareness of it. This work of remembering requires discipline and prayerful attentiveness, but it is clarifying and validating to have someone listening deeply to my story and inviting me to reflect further. As I gather the threads of my life and speak them aloud to another, I am amazed by how mysterious and wonderful it is to have been called into being at all. It is rare to be given the opportunity to reflect in this way, and I am grateful for it.

Endnotes

1 Buechner, Frederick. *A Room Called Remember: Uncollected Pieces.* New York: Harper Collins, 1984, 6.

II

"Let's all do it," said Mr. Watts. "Close your eyes and silently recite your name."

The sound of my name took me to a place deep inside my head. I already knew that words could take you into a new world, but I didn't know that on the strength of one word spoken for my ears only I would find myself in a room that no one else knew about...

"Another thing," Mr. Watts said. "No one in the history of your short lives has used the same voice as you with which to say your name. This is yours. Your special gift that no one can ever take from you."

Lloyd Jones, *Mr Pip* [1]

Awakening

Fear not: for I have redeemed thee, I have called thee by thy name, thou art mine. When thou passest through the waters, I will be with thee, and through the rivers they shall not overflow thee.

Isaiah 43:1–2 KJV

My parents named me grandly—Eugene Lincoln Napoleon Veith. This choice of names reflects my parents' interest in world affairs and my father's pride in his beloved French heritage. I think they also suggest some of the qualities my parents admired, and perhaps their hope that something of the spirit of these great men might be found in me as I grew up. Certainly I have always taken a keen interest in the lives of those after whom I was named, and looking back, I am becoming even more conscious of the influence these names have had on my life.

"Eugene" recalls the son of the Empress Josephine by her first marriage.[2] She later became the wife of Napoleon, who was a hero of my father and grandfather and whose life is also revered in the choice of "Napoleon" as my third name.[3] "Lincoln" recalls the great American President who freed the slaves.[4]

I was the fourth son born into the family and was followed by a daughter and another son, making six children in all. My parents had little money and life must often have seemed very daunting to them. Nevertheless, they were people of courage and faith and we knew ourselves to be deeply loved.

I was born into tumultuous times. In 1915, the first World War was gathering destructive momentum. Australia was a fledgling nation of barely fourteen years, following the Federation of the various States in January1901. There were great challenges. Passions were running high on the issue of conscription; a terrible drought brought widespread hardship to many communities and thousands of young men and women left the country for active service overseas, while at home their elders and younger siblings tried to hold things together in other costly ways.

A few short months before my birth, the Anzacs had landed at Gallipoli, an event which has unfolded in amazing ways within our national memory. When my lusty birth cries filled the delivery room of Box Hill hospital in one of Melbourne's outer eastern suburbs, no one dreamed that the impossible odds faced by the young Australian and New Zealand soldiers trying to gain a foothold on the coast of Turkey would become one of the great symbols of what it now means to be an Australian. Back then, it was just another difficult issue to occupy the attention of the people and their politicians.

I remember nothing of all this, of course, but I was born into the hopes and terrors of this time and imbibed them with my mother's milk. Now I look back and feel how hard it must have been for my young parents, as for all their contemporaries, and I am touched by their courage and hope in bringing babies into the world at such a time. Their families came from France, Ireland and England and the richness of this mixed heritage seeped into my siblings and me from our earliest childhood.

My grandparents on my father's side were Charles and Rosanna (nee Bammer) Veith. They were married at Chalmers Manse in East Melbourne on March 10, 1863. Their marriage certificate indicates that they were thirty and twenty-four years old respectively, and that neither had been married before. He was born in Paris, France in 1833 and she in Belfast, Ireland in 1839. Charles' profession is noted as butcher.

Family anecdotes maintain they met each other in dramatic circumstances. Rosanna, whose family lived in a castle, was engaged to be married to an English gentleman who had come to Australia in the early days of the gold rushes. She made the long, tedious voyage from Ireland in order to marry him, but when the ship berthed, he was not there to meet her because a dreadful flood hindered him from arriving in time. There was no way of contacting her with this news and Rosanna was extremely upset. Angry and fearful, she declared that she would marry the first man who asked her. This man was CharlesVeith. Whatever happened to the unfortunate Englishman, I don't know!

Charles was an ardent Frenchman, a tall young man who had been an officer in the Imperial Army of Napoleon III. [5] He was a great admirer of Napoleon Bonaparte, an admiration which filtered down through the generations and found expression in my third name. His restless energy soon had him leaving France and travelling the world. Eventually, his taste for adventure brought him to Australia in the early days of the gold rushes. At the time of his marriage to Rosanna he was living in Chewton, a small town near Bendigo, which was the centre for several of the gold fields.

Eugene's grandfather Charles Veith - courtesy of the Veith family

Charles and Rosanna were an adventurous couple, and they had seven children, of whom six survived. Their first child, a son, was born at Chewton in Victoria in 1864. Sometime later, possibly after the second child's death at a very young age, the family went to New Zealand. The remaining five children, including my father, Charles, the sixth child in the family and the second boy, were probably all born in New Zealand, though it has been difficult to get accurate records. The family remained in New Zealand at least until 1878, when their youngest child was born in Auckland.[6]

My grandfather seems to have had several successful business interests. At the time of the youngest child's birth, he listed his profession as a boarding house keeper, though all previous documentation refers to his profession as a butcher. He also owned gold mines in New Zealand. Everything he put his hand to seemed to prosper, and at one time he was reputed to be the richest man in the country. The family lived in comfort and style, with servants and nannies, befitting their wealth.

Perhaps Charles' restlessness and love of travel prompted him to relocate his family to Fiji, where he became a well-known and highly regarded hotel keeper. His photo appears in a museum in Suva amongst records of early European settlers. Around the late 1880s or early 1890s, the family returned to Melbourne, Australia, maybe attracted by the boom period captured in the famous "Marvellous Melbourne" slogan that invited settlers from around the world. Here, Charles resumed his occupation as a butcher. One family story tells how he used to deliver meat to his customers in Melbourne riding an old circus horse and once, as he was riding along, a band began playing in the street and the horse started dancing!

My grandfather was flamboyant, outgoing and generous, alleged to have spoken seven languages fluently. He never lost his exuberant love for France and all things French and the culture, language, manners and cuisine of France were central features of my grandparents' home environment. Mealtime conversations were conducted in French and no doubt Napoleon Bonaparte often featured in these. This fervent Frenchness was embraced by my father as he grew up and certainly passed on to me in both my name and in many other ways. I remember learning as a very small boy that I must always stand when a lady entered the room and formally bow to her in greeting. If I met a lady I knew when I was outside, I was aware that I must behave as all the other men in my family did, always raising my hat and bowing in greeting and respect. These are customs I still keep now. They are part of who I am.

But my grandfather's interests also extended far beyond the borders of France and all his life he maintained a lively interest in world affairs in spite of living so far from Europe. He ensured that his children attended good schools and habitually drew them into discussions about world affairs, music and the arts. My father absorbed all this and passed on to me a similar interest which I carry to this day. My grand name captures this wider family context as well as the more immediate choice of my parents.

Unfortunately, grandfather Charles, who was so outgoing and generous, grew into a heavy gambler, and the family fortune was eventually dissipated. This change in circumstances must have been very hard for them, particularly my grandparents, whose marriage surely suffered from the strain. The children all had to find jobs, some of them in factories. My father, Charles, learned the trade of butchering, as his father had, and also farming. When his brother died in his early thirties, he was left as the only son in a family of four surviving daughters.

Though my grandfather was not a man of faith, the misfortunes that came upon the family caused them to look for a deeper meaning in life and to realise that wealth was not all that important. Eventually, most of them became Christians and friendly neighbours invited them to the Church of Christ in Brighton, a move which proved to be of great significance for it was in this community of faith that my parents met.

Eugene's parents Charles and Laura Veith - courtesy of the Veith family

Family stories tell how my father Charles fell in love with a young woman called Laura Rosalie Day when he saw her sitting underneath an apple tree. They married on September 19, 1906, when Charles was twenty-eight and Laura was twenty-six. Her profession is noted as homemaker and his as butcher. Neither of them was previously married.

My mother's parents were Charles Day, an accountant, and Susannah Durrant. They married in Brighton, Melbourne in 1879. Both sets of her grandparents came from England—the Days from Dewsbury near York and the Durrants from Sussex. Her Durrant grandparents had met and married in Melbourne in 1847, making them some of the early settlers in Melbourne, which at that time was still part of the colony of New South Wales.

My mother's father died when he was quite young, leaving her mother with a house and four children, two boys and two girls, but no income. This was extremely hard for her and she worked long hours to support the family by sewing. In order to ease the strain, my mother was adopted by her uncle and aunt who were successful in business but had no children of their own. Laura thus entered into a very different lifestyle from her siblings. She was brought up in luxury, riding in a carriage with her adopted parents, used to servants and quite without the stress of very limited finances. But then everything changed for her again. Her uncle died when she was twelve years old, and three years later her aunt died, leaving all her money to a religious group in America.

Laura returned to her mother's home where she had to earn her keep and help the family income by sewing. Once more she was one of four siblings in straitened circumstances, which must have involved big readjustments for them all. Her brothers loved her dearly, but the family soon farewelled one of them to America, and the other to the goldfields. Laura's mother and her two daughters were left to negotiate another new configuration of their family. The sisters were very aware of their different upbringings, but tolerance and kindness prevailed where friction could have crept in and the household managed the big changes. Thus when Charles and Laura fell in love, they had each already experienced both wealth and poverty and they knew well the challenges of starting all over again.

My parents were very different people, yet their marriage was happy. My father was intelligent, exuberant, charming, a great raconteur and a welcome guest on social occasions. He enjoyed telling the stories he had heard from his father about his adventurous life in Napoleon III's army, followed by years of wandering the world, as well as telling his own tales of his childhood years in New Zealand and Fiji. My father imbibed from his father an intense interest in international affairs and an insatiable thirst for knowledge, which he passed on to me. Though he was impetuous and somewhat unstable like his father, he was a good man who loved my mother exceedingly.

Unlike my father's flamboyance, my mother had an English reticence and a quiet personality. Perhaps that is why the two of them got on so well together. She influenced me more than anyone else, both as a child and as an adult. Her gentle, loving temperament had a gracious effect upon me and many others. People really loved her and appreciated her depth of character and kindness. She had a penetrating, intuitive mind and was very discerning of people and situations.

By a strange coincidence, her family also had connections to Napoleon. They fought against him in the English army. We had a number of British mementos from the Napoleonic era in our home, which my mother greatly treasured: a family seal which had belonged to one of her forebears, who was an aide-de-compte to the Duke of Wellington at the battle of Waterloo;[7] a little writing desk with a secret drawer that was used during that famous battle; and a silver spoon with the name of my ancestor's battalion on it. She passed these special things on to my older brother and me upon her death. I don't know how she felt about the adulation of Napoleon by my father and grandfather, but I suspect that it was our good fortune that she had such a quiet, calm and loving disposition, or we may have had the Napoleonic wars continued in our home!

As a young man, my father learned farming and the butchery trade, but his first job was at the relatively new retail firm of Myer in Melbourne. He knew Sidney Myer, the founder of this famous business, very well. But in spite of this steady job, he hankered after running his own business and decided to move into farming. He accepted a position as manager of a 320-acre farm at Yarragon South in Central Gippsland, Victoria. As soon as my mother had recovered from my birth, when I was six weeks old, he moved our family away from the city to the farm. I was the fourth son, and my three older brothers—Charles, Louis and Walter—were seven, five and three. My brother Charles remembered that our family travelled by train to Yarragon and from there negotiated the three miles to the farm by walking behind a horse-drawn vehicle containing the bare necessities of our furniture and household goods and perhaps the younger children as well. I imagine the journey must have been very difficult for them all.

***

The farm was on the northern slopes of the Strzelecki Ranges, three miles from the town of Yarragon, which is situated between the townships of Warragul and Trafalgar. Interestingly, I recently learned that Yarragon was originally called Waterloo, because of its proximity to the town of Trafalgar—a strange coincidence! The farm was used primarily to graze sheep, but the country was hilly and difficult to work. My father's salary was one pound, ten shillings a week, a rent-free house and the right to cultivate five acres of the land for his own use. Much of the farm was covered with bracken fern, blackberries and tussocks, but there were substantial areas of pasture too.

Our farmhouse was a weatherboard with four rooms—a kitchen, living room and two bedrooms, the walls of which were lined with hessian, as were the ceilings. There was no electricity, bathroom, or laundry, and the washing was done in a copper tub over a wood fire out in the open. There was a one-thousand gallon tank, which caught the rainwater from the roof, and at first it was necessary to go outside to get water, but later a pipe was installed to bring this into the kitchen. There was no radio or telephone, and the main source of information was the daily newspaper and the "Weekly Times" for farmers.

My two younger siblings, Olive and Arthur, were born after we arrived on the farm,[8] and we all worked very hard. There was milking to be done every morning and evening. Each weekday, we walked the two-and-a-half miles to our school, though occasionally I was allowed to ride one of the horses if it could be spared. I was very fond of the horses and greatly enjoyed riding, which I did well—it was my main interest during those years. The school consisted of three rooms and was staffed by four teachers, including the headmaster.

Eugene with his older brothers
Left to right – Louis (12) Charles (15) Walter (8) Seated, Eugene (5)
in 1920 - courtesy of the Veith family

After school, there were many chores—milking the cows, cutting ferns, and setting traps for rabbits, which were there in plague proportions and had to be culled continually. Apart from the occasional shin of beef, they were our source of meat. We ate them in as many different ways as my mother could imagine—boiled, stewed, roasted, fried—but always rabbit. Our other staple was the potatoes we grew, and we had plenty of milk and eggs. Although nourishing, our diet was monotonous and lacked fresh fruit and green vegetables, though we did have limited supplies of watercress, which grew along the banks of the creek in summertime. We also had fresh lemons, which we picked up from the ground where they had fallen from a beautiful lemon tree, whose branches overhung the fence of a property we walked past on our way home from school. Our own fruit trees were not so bountiful, except for the cherry plum and quince. As babies and young children we were never seriously ill. I am sure that my mother would have claimed that this was at least partly due to "Babies Blessing," a herbal mixture prepared and sold by Broadbent and Sons, well-known herbalists in Melbourne. Although we were extremely poor and always poorly clothed, we did not go hungry. But there were not many luxuries—even at Christmastime, we only received a few boiled lollies in a Christmas stocking.

Probably on the farm at Yarragon - courtesy of the Veith family

Farming the potatoes was backbreaking work. First there was the planting, then the harvesting and finally the marketing, provided the crop was not ruined in some way by potato blight or other disasters, which sometimes happened. All of them had to be hand lifted from the ground by fork, then gathered together and put in hessian sacks. Each sack weighed at least one hundredweight (112 pounds or about 50 kilograms), making handling these no easy task. Milking the cows by hand was not hard work like that, but it was tedious and never-ending—twice daily, every day.

Even though my childhood years on the farm were marked by poverty and hard work and life was a continual struggle for us, I remember that time with a great deal of pleasure. Growing up, we shared a lot of warmth and love as a family, and we expressed our affection for each other in very overt ways. We all knew that we were loved. We were very happy together, and we were also surrounded by the beauty of nature—lovely trees, many diverse birds, wild deer and a very large pond, where we children had a raft which we played on for hours. We loved the exhilaration of sliding down grassy hills on sheets of iron, like skis or toboggans. We had endless enjoyment from simple things like this, and we seldom had any fights apart from the fun of pillow fights. I don't remember us ever getting nasty with each other and I suppose this was due to our parents' influence and example.

Sometimes cousins, uncles and aunts would come to stay with us over the New Year period, bringing with them much excitement and new possibilities. During these visits, the children had fun sleeping outside in tents. We amused ourselves in all sorts of ways, one of which was to ride down a very steep hill on a sort of billy cart. It was a two axle, four wheel contraption on which only one person could sit. It was steered by placing both feet on the moveable front axle. The brake was an engineering masterpiece, consisting of a thick stick fastened through a slit in the seat. When the top of the stick was pushed forward, it would clear the ground underneath; when pulled back, it would make contact with the ground and hopefully act as an effective brake. The whole contraption was very unstable and hazardous, but that's what made it such good fun. As the cart sped downhill, the rider usually fell off, but little harm was done because the vehicle was close to the ground. There were extra squeals of delight when one of the adults fell off.

A highlight of these visits would be a journey to Allambee deep in the Strezlecki Ranges.[9] We travelled there in the jinker and the springcart or on horseback. There were majestic stands of mountain ash trees, hundreds of feet high. Flocks of bright red parrots nested in the tall trees and flew about with wonderful grace. Blackberries grew prolifically in the open spaces, and we would collect the berries and return home laden with them to enjoy eating them fresh with scones and cream. The rest would be made into jam. It was a wonderful adventure that we talked about for many months.

We made a lot of jam in those days—cherry plum and melon, as well as blackberry. It was all prepared in the same way. The fruit was cut into small pieces, then mixed one pound of fruit to one pound of sugar. We stored the jam in any old bottles we could find. To remove the neck of a bottle, we dipped a thin string of wool into kerosene and wrapped it around the bottle just below the neck. Then we lit the wool with a match and a few seconds later dipped the bottle into a bucket of cold water. The top of the bottle came off cleanly, just where the wool had been. After filling the bottle with jam, we covered it with brown paper soaked in a solution of flour and water to make it stick.

When I was about seven years old, I received my first book, and it became one of my greatest treasures. Because we had very few extras, it was significant that I received a book at this young age, particularly since the book was Abbott's *Life of Napoleon Bonaparte,* which probably has as many words and chapters as the Bible! I took a special interest in Napoleon because of my name and because he was such a hero to my father and grandfather. The book was very pro-Napoleon—unlike the history teacher and books at school, which were biased against Napoleon and naturally favoured the English. Even though I was painfully shy and stammered as a child, I spoke out vehemently in class on behalf of Napoleon, arguing my case against the teacher.

Since then, I have built up a whole library on Napoleon and the French history of that time and I have come to a much more balanced view of both. My name and that first book led me to a lifelong interest in French history and culture, which was already part of my family heritage. I began to make it my own. The thread of France through my life has enriched me immensely, opening me up to the knowledge and experience of another land and culture to which I feel attached at a deep level.

These happy experiences of my childhood shaped my life in many ways, but I also remember my parents' constant struggle to make ends meet and their longing to achieve my father's dream of running the farm successfully—a goal that finally eluded them, as he was not a good farmer from the business point of view, although he was creative and he did invent several things. I can still feel the sorrow and helplessness I felt as a child as I sensed my parents straining beneath the burden and anxiety of managing the farm. My feelings about these harsher realities gradually developed into my lifelong concern for those trapped in burdensome cycles of poverty, and I am poignantly aware of how the struggles of my parents during the Yarragon years planted seeds of vision and an energy for change within me.

Though I was largely unaware of this at the time, I do still remember a vivid dream in which I saw myself as a grown-up person handing out a lot of money to people who needed it. When I woke up, I said, "I don't believe it. That will never happen." Even though I dismissed the dream as completely impossible, I never forgot it, or the effect it had on me. It seemed to bring together the paradox of the hardships and the blessings that I experienced growing up on the farm, and it captured my early yearning to help relieve those who were suffering from the oppression of entrenched poverty. There were many other seeds sown within me during those years, but why some took root rather than others remains hidden in the mystery of how God's Spirit lives within us and the ways we respond.

* * *

Like so much else of significance in my life, the genesis of my knowing God's loving and healing presence lies in my early years on the Yarragon farm. I am realising more and more how much of the person I have become is grounded in those experiences, even though I don't recall thinking much about God or having a personal faith at all as a child. I guess that like many children, I tended to take my life for granted, including my parents and God. This is interesting to notice now, because my faith and experience of God has been so central for the rest of my life.

I do remember praying together as a family, both for healing and also when my father felt under pressure. As a young man, he had experienced healing prayer for a very serious illness and his recovery made a lasting impression on him. He often recalled his enthusiasm when he was first converted and how he would stay up all night reading the Word and praying. He was also very convinced of the importance of fasting when praying deeply about something. This and his interest in the Second Coming of Christ were his two great convictions and the main spiritual food we received. During these times, he exhibited great faith and prayed deeply, but in between these intense seasons, he would get side-tracked into other interests, and his faith would recede into the background.

Though my father was a keen student of the Word, family Bible studies were a bit erratic. Sometimes my parents invited neighbours to join them in Bible study on a Sunday, but we did not attend church while we were living on the farm, so we had no regular faith community which nurtured us in faith or gave us a sense of belonging and support. This was partly because my father was not impressed with the two churches in Yarragon, the Methodists and the Church of England, which he thought were pretty dead. Moreover, attending church regularly would have been difficult for our family, since we were tied to the night and morning milking routine every day, and it was a three-mile journey in the horse and jinker to these churches. My mother said very little about God that I can remember, but she lived her faith quietly and consistently in gentle, unobtrusive ways that I only recognised when I grew older. She had a great depth to her and was very loving and unselfish. Scarcely a day goes by that I don't remember her and thank God for her. Looking back, I wonder what sustained my parents' faith during those hard years on the farm.

But my parents taught us about the Lord, and as a child I had a simple acceptance of what they said. I believed that God had created the world and loved us. I also had an awareness of prayer and the healing power of God. Once, when my father borrowed a horse from a neighbour in order to do some job on the farm, it got into the clover patch and had a feast. As a result, its stomach became extremely bloated, and throughout the night the poor animal was in extreme agony. We were all very distressed, both for the horse's suffering and because it did not belong to us. Our parents were very afraid that the horse would die, causing considerable hardship for both our family and our neighbours'. We all prayed earnestly for the horse to be healed, and in the morning it was quite all right. That incident impressed me and encouraged me to keep exploring healing prayer.

On another occasion, my young sister Olive was running around the yard with a tin whistle in her mouth, having a wonderful time, until she tripped and fell. The whistle pierced the roof of her mouth, cutting away a big piece of the flesh. In great distress, our family gathered around her and prayed for healing, because the nearest doctor was fifteen miles from the farm—a long journey with a horse and jinker that was very difficult with an injured person. The next morning, when we looked into her mouth with trepidation, the flesh had closed, and we saw only the faintest trace of a scar.

Eugene's father Charles and only sister Olive - courtesy of the Veith family

I also vividly recall the day when my older brother Charlie was splitting wood—one of his daily chores—and I was running around outside, letting off steam and not looking where I was going. As he swung his newly sharpened axe downward, I ran too close to him, and the blade came down on my face, slicing my nose so that it hung down over my mouth. Charlie ran to my mother, who urgently summoned my father. My nose was pushed back into place and held there, whilst they worked out how to get me to the nearest doctor, who was miles away at Trafalgar. The jinker was the only appropriate means of travel under such circumstances, but the fastest and most reliable horse was Molly, who was only used for riding and had never been broken into harness, a task that normally took days, sometimes weeks. Speed, however, was of the essence, and father harnessed Molly to the jinker, kept a very firm grip of the reins, and urged her forward. His confidence in her was rewarded, as she maintained a very fast pace all the way, ensuring that I received the prompt medical attention I needed. He felt this was an answer to prayer. When we arrived, the doctor stitched my nose back into place without any anaesthetic, while several nurses held me down on the table until the ordeal was over.[10] Looking back, I am amazed at how well everything healed and also how fortunate I was that the axe did not do more permanent damage to my face.

Now that I am a parent, grandparent and great-grandparent, I am much more aware of the fear, remorse and tentative faith my parents must have felt as they lived through this traumatic incident. As I recall the event, I feel immense gratitude for the physical healing I experienced, though ever since the accident I have had trouble with my speech. Even though this difficulty is largely overcome, I still stammer and often have to hesitate when I am speaking because the right word is frequently hard for me to pronounce, and I have to think carefully of a substitute that may be easier for me to say.

When the Great Depression hit, our life on the farm became too difficult. My father was not a natural businessman like my grandfather, and he made some foolish decisions with regard to the farm, which exacerbated the more inherent difficulties with the place. This defeat was disheartening and disappointing for my parents and when I was eleven or twelve years old, my father decided to take us back to the city and try to find work that would support our family.

I'll never forget my life at Yarragon, even though at the time I took it all for granted. Our family was emotionally secure and embedded in a faith that enfolded us. We were surrounded by great natural beauty and spaciousness. And we were happy. The harsh difficulties and anxieties of our life then sowed seeds of compassion and resilience in me, which have influenced my life choices and direction. Now, savouring these memories as an adult, I feel gratitude welling up in me for the love and faith of my parents, which pervaded everything and has sustained me throughout my life.

* * *

From Yarragon, we moved to Kensington,[11] where I attended the state school. On the verge of adolescence, I suddenly became a "country bumpkin," totally unaccustomed to life in suburban Melbourne. I was also highly sensitive, stuttered badly and was starting to lose my hair, a daunting combination of realities that accompanied my newcomer status in the city school. The boys seemed a wild lot to me, and I was intimidated by them. They, in turn, must have found me an oddball, and they tormented me in excruciating ways. So I hated school, and my studies suffered badly as a result of my distress.

Then my father was offered a loan to start a butcher's shop in Glenferrie Road, Malvern. This move away from a painful place and peer group appealed to me, particularly since my older brother and I were invited to help our father run the business and learn the trade of butchering, as he and my grandfather had done. In order to leave school after the exams, before I had quite obtained the legal age of fourteen for compulsory schooling, my parents had to get permission from the Education Department. Knowing the ordeal was coming to an end, I was able to relax, and my school work improved greatly. When I finally left Kensington, I was near the top of the class, which was a source of great satisfaction to me and my parents.

In Malvern, we lived above the butcher's shop and began to worship at Armadale Baptist Church. This marked a new time for us all. As our family began to share life with this faith community, we were encouraged to make a serious commitment to Jesus and this emphasis touched me deeply. I attended the Boys Brigade club which I enjoyed and made a new group of friends but I also received valuable teaching and support from Mr Evans, the minister, as well as Gordon Williams from the nearby

Brethren Assembly. Both men taught, encouraged and guided me through my developing relationship with God, and their influence on me has been profound.

The Veith butcher shop in Malvern - courtesy of the Veith family

My father employed Gordon Williams from time to time, and he took a special interest in me. Through his example and witness, I became aware of my need for God and longed for a personal relationship with Jesus. When I was fourteen or fifteen, I became conscious that God was dealing with me. That is perhaps an odd way of putting it, but it expresses my feeling that God was drawing me, nudging me, encouraging me towards a committed relationship. And I came to understand that the Lord was someone I wanted to love. Without any fanfare, or any particular moment marking this as a momentous occasion, I found myself intentionally committing myself to Jesus Christ and his way of faith and life.

Yet these were tumultuous years for me, because I found it difficult to feel sure that I was actually following Jesus. In the language of the time, I lacked assurance. One day I felt like a Christian, and the next I did not.

It was very painful. I longed for the Lord and sought him, but I wasn't sure I had really found him. I relied heavily on my feelings and had the swinging emotions of a teenager regarding my faith as well as most other things. Gordon helped me through this roller coaster of confused feelings. Gradually, I began to realise that my feelings were not a completely reliable indicator of my relationship with the Lord. I had grown up hearing a lot of rather dramatic conversion stories, and I think I thought that my experience was not valid because it was very ordinary and undramatic. So I had to learn that for some people, faith was a simple matter of accepting God and what he says in his Word. To begin my journey of knowing God, I had to stop looking for dramatic feelings.

I remember picking up a tract about a person who had this same problem, and it proved to be a great help to me. The author remarked that when you learn to swim, you must eventually trust yourself to the water or you'll never get started, but will keep on sinking. In the life of faith, you must first trust what God says, and then you will begin to receive assurance. I was expecting to receive assurance of God's presence in my life before I trusted God. As a matter of fact, I did find it very hard to learn to swim, because for a long time I could not trust myself to the water. Eventually, after much painful struggle and questioning, I began to surrender my swinging emotions to God, rather than seeing them as an indication of God's presence or absence in my life, or a reflection of my commitment to God. When I was seventeen years old, I made this decision firmly and held to it. From that time on, my uneasiness over the state of my soul disappeared, and I received the assurance of salvation that I had so desired. Since then, I haven't even thought about it.

Through this experience, I have come to understand that it is necessary to "mean business with the Lord."[12] Though I didn't use this phrase at the time of my initial youthful surrender to the Lord, it captures my sense of a serious commitment to the ways of God and a genuine, deep desire for God, which is essential for a growth in the knowledge and love of God. Through my many years of experience in the business world, this phrase has become very meaningful for me. Meaning business is meaning to do as you say—to be "fair dinkum" to use a popular Australian expression. You don't get far in business if you keep changing your mind, breaking your word, evading your commitments, playing games, not being genuine.

Of course, you don't get far in anything if you do those things! I've also found that it is possible to deceive myself by saying I mean business, but not actually following through with it. Eventually, I realise that I have to be more honest with myself and ask: "Do I really mean business about this or not?" It's a good, honest question that guides me.

After this foundational commitment to the Lord and the joy of my subsequent baptism, I had an avid desire to grow in my relationship with God. Along with helping in the butcher's shop, I delivered meat orders to our customers on my bicycle. On top of the parcels of meat that I packed in the basket on the front of my bike, I balanced my open Bible so that I could memorise scriptures and the promises of God as I travelled. Sometimes I read other books as I cycled along, eager to devour everything I could that would encourage my faith. How different that time was from today—and not only in the amount of traffic on the road! I cannot picture a teenager reading the Bible while riding around on a bike now.

During my years of apprenticing in my father's butcher's shop, we were settled in a nurturing community of faith, and I had discovered the peace and joy of God in my life, which was a marvellous gift after my years of angst and struggle. As I read and pursued my interests in learning about faith and world affairs, my life seemed secure and expansive, something I had not experienced since leaving the farm.

But alongside my emerging sense of well-being, I was painfully shy and almost totally lacking in self-confidence. My childhood stammer had become a serious problem and pervaded everything. Throughout my teens, I could not answer the phone because I knew that I would be unable to speak. When I travelled on the trams, as I had to do frequently, I always made sure I had the exact money for the fare so that I would not have to say anything. Once, when I had to buy a rail ticket, there was a long queue behind me and the train was coming, but I was unable to speak. To this day, I can feel the fear and humiliation rising in me when I recall this dreadful incident. Only those who have suffered similar impediments can understand the excruciating agony of these embarrassing experiences.

* * *

During this time of heightened sensitivity, self-consciousness and general awkwardness as I transitioned from childhood to young adulthood, I was not only tormented by my stammer, but also by the bald patches that began to appear on my head. Though my hair sometimes grew again, the bald patches continued their relentless march across my scalp. In desperation, I began rubbing black crayon onto my scalp, but this did not assuage the sick feeling of helplessness and heartache that enveloped me. This creeping hair loss was caused by a condition called *alopecia universalis* ("hair loss over the entire body"), which meant that eventually I would have no hair anywhere on my body—not even eyelashes or eyebrows. Though this was an accurate medical description for what was happening to me, it seemed ludicrously inadequate to describe my feeling of impending disaster. Unlike my peers, I would never shave. With my stammer and my weirdly spreading baldness, I stood out from them in visible and humiliating ways and was unable to hide myself comfortably within a peer group.

Because the baldness was so unexpected and gradual, I was always hoping that it had stopped. The hair would regrow for a time, and I would think my prayers had been answered. Then it would fall out again—and I would pray desperately that it would get better. For a time, it would seem to do so, only to fall out again with relentless repetition. I lived with a constant rising and then falling of hope, which was enervating and disheartening. I hated it—and I also hated the way people stared at me. I'd go into a restaurant and would see all the children looking at me and would hear them say to their mother, "Look over there...that man's got no hair...Look at him, Mum. What's wrong with him?"

With cortisone treatments, my hair grew back, but very thinly—and the side-effects were so bad that I did not continue with the medication. Then I went to a clinic where special oils were rubbed into my scalp with the accompanying assurance that the hair would regrow. Instead, it removed what little hair I had remaining—and so, since my early thirties, I've been completely and inexorably bald.

As an old man, I've come to terms with the universal baldness of my body. Most of the time, I forget about it altogether, because I merge naturally with my bald peers instead of standing out from them in the painful way I did as a young man. Though this was very traumatic for me as a youth, I tried to make light of it in public. Faced with the oddity of my totally bald head atop a still youthful face, I told my friends: "Just call me Curly!" And to help bridge the awkwardness of my looks when meeting someone for the first time, I'd smile and say, "Just call me Curly." The humour worked, and "Curly" quickly became my nickname—and an affectionate one at that. Later on, as hairpieces began to look less artificial, I tried them in a bid to solve this problem, but I have been very self-conscious about that too.[13]

During those formative years in the butcher's shop, the seeds of healing prayer that had been planted in me while living on the farm began to grow. My newfound trust in God and his promises ignited my interest in divine healing, both because of my own daunting health problems and also those of people around me. During this time, I came under the influence of some people who were enthusiastic exponents of divine healing. They believed strongly that healing "was in the atonement," as they put it, and that if they had sufficient faith, God would certainly heal them. They would not go to doctors and spoke of them disparagingly as unnecessary for those with sufficient faith.

This attitude made me uneasy, but I was young and inexperienced and drawn to the idea of God healing people. Yet I soon grew increasingly doubtful, especially about the idea that we did not need doctors. But in that milieu, to doubt signalled a lack of faith, so when my doubts grew, it was a very confusing and uncomfortable time for me. I felt inwardly torn between my desire to grow in faith, as it was being presented to me, and my burgeoning commonsense and questioning mind. When I started questioning the teaching, I worried that I was lacking in faith, and this put my mind and emotions into turmoil.

Eventually, things clarified very quickly when one of the people in the group influenced a woman who became ill to refuse to see a doctor. When her condition worsened, she eventually asked for one to come, but it was too late, and she died the following day. Her parents, who were not believers, were naturally extremely upset about the whole event and put the matter into the hands of lawyers. This was a terrible tragedy for the woman and her family, and I was greatly shocked and realised that this understanding of divine healing was unbalanced and extreme. I left the group and began to pay more careful attention to my feelings of uneasiness in other situations. This experience sparked my desire to grow in the art of discernment, particularly in matters of faith. Yet because I had very low self-esteem, no self-confidence and assumed that feelings were not important, especially for young men, this early glimmer of wisdom was hard for me to follow.

Around this time, shortly after I turned eighteen, my father became very ill and the business had to be sold so that he could recuperate. During the early years of the Great Depression, business in general struggled but even so, father generously supplied many of our relatives with meat that they could not afford to buy and he was always very helpful to customers who had trouble paying their accounts. But as with the farm, he was not a good businessman, and the stress of trying to make the shop a viable business must have contributed significantly to his ill-health. From this vulnerable position, our family had to figure out how to survive. I had left school before I was fourteen and had not yet fully learned the butchering trade. Moreover, the Great Depression continued, unemployment was rampant and employment extremely difficult to find, particularly with my low self-confidence.

After everything else was sold, our family retained a broken-down Austin 7—"a baby Austin"—that didn't even have a door on the driver's side. I had a cousin working in Flinders Lane, Melbourne, for a firm called Scott Brothers, and he suggested that there might be an opportunity for doing transport deliveries with them. With no other possibility before me and having just gained my driver's licence, I set out to find a job in order to help ease the strain on the family. Of course, I had no inkling then that this small opening would lead me to establish a parcel transport business which would eventually become the largest capital city metro parcel organisation in the country, generating a very significant income and opening avenues of Christian service that I could never have imagined in my wildest dreams.

Though I have overcome the crippling effects of my stammering and have confronted my hair loss with humour, the shadow of these afflictions continues to hover around me. Even now, when I am tired, the stammer tends to return, and I have always found it hard to express myself, even though I would have liked so much to be good at this. Because I had to leave school not long before my fourteenth birthday, I have felt my educational inadequacy very keenly all my life. Perhaps this is why I continue to read newspapers and magazines for two or three hours each day, a habit that has given me a general knowledge of world affairs.

I have led an active life in the church and the world, raised a family, travelled extensively, and had interesting engagements with many people around the world—all involving many phone calls, board meetings, public speaking occasions, and pastoral exchanges. Yet as I have sat in meetings with very intelligent, well-educated people, I have sometimes realised to my surprise that they are unaware of certain aspects of life that are very familiar to me, and their ignorance in these areas amazes me. Life is a funny mix. We are all inadequate in different ways; we are all ignorant in different ways.

As I remember myself now as a shy, balding stammering teenager, the journey seems miraculous. I am interested in going back over my earlier years and trying to capture the source of my later struggles and growth in faith and my deepening awareness of God's loving presence in everything. I am noticing so much more as I take my time to stop and reflect. That's one of the advantages of growing old—looking back over a long life and taking a long view of things, seeing now what I could not see when I was younger.

Endnotes

1 Jones, Lloyd. *Mister Pip*. Melbourne: Text, 2007, 108.

2 Eugene de Beauharnais, Napoleon's stepson, whom he adopted. Even so, he was not eligible to inherit the imperial throne. A gifted tactician, Eugene commanded the Army of Italy and served as viceroy of Italy for Napoleon. In this capacity, he enacted many liberal constitutional reforms.

3 Napoleon Bonaparte was born on August 15, 1769, in Corsica, France. One of the most celebrated leaders in the history of the West, he revolutionized military organization and training, re-organised education, sponsored the Napoleonic Code (the French civil code enacted in 1804), which also became the prototype of later civil law codes in Europe and Latin America, and established the long-standing Concordat with the papacy, which defined the status of the Roman Catholic church in France and ended the divisions caused by church reforms and confiscation during the French Revolution. He died on May 5, 1821 on the island of St. Helena in the South Atlantic Ocean.

4 Abraham Lincoln is regarded as one of America's greatest heroes. He grew up in a log cabin in rural Kentucky in a family that struggled with poverty and death. From these humble beginnings, he was inaugurated as the sixteenth President of the United States in March 1861. In 1863, he issued the Emancipation Proclamation abolishing slavery, and he was assassinated in April 1865. His short Presidency spanned the Civil War years and included his famous Gettysburg Address, which honoured the war dead and stated boldly: "that we here resolve that these dead shall not have died in vain—that this nation, under God, shall have a new birth of freedom—and that government of the people, by the people, for the people, shall not perish from the earth."

5 Louis-Napoléon Bonaparte was the nephew of Napoleon I (Napoleon Bonaparte). He was the first President of the French Second Republic and as Napoleon III, he was the Emperor of the Second French Empire.

6 The children of Charles and Rosanna Veith: Edmond, Laura, Rose, Isabel, Jane Amelia, Charles, Josephine. The first two were born in Victoria, Australia; the others most probably in New Zealand.

7 The Battle of Waterloo was fought close to Brussels in 1815 between the French (under the command of Napoleon Bonaparte) and the Allied armies (commanded by the Duke of Wellington from Britain and General Blücher from Prussia). The French defeat at Waterloo drew to a close twenty-three years of war, beginning with the French Revolutionary wars in 1792 and continuing with the Napoleonic Wars from 1803. Napoleon's defeat at Waterloo marked the end of his last bid for power. He was exiled to the island of St Helena and died in 1821.

8 In his unpublished personal story, *Life on the Farm*, Eugene's oldest brother, Charles, recalled incidents of that time. One of these was his father's great excitement and joy at the birth of Olive in 1918: "Father desperately wanted a daughter, especially after four boys. Mother was sent to Melbourne (Brighton) for the confinement. Immediately he got news of the great event he drafted a telegram to Mother and sent me off to the Post Office to send it. I cannot recall the wording of the telegram, but Father, in his excitement and joy, must have used some extravagant language because the postmistress questioned me on it and said something to the effect that it was a most unusual message."

9 Charles notes a further memory about how the family leased a better farm at Allambee, with high hopes of an improved life. He describes the Sunday school class his father organised there for a short period and the drama of a bushfire which threatened their home. The move was short-lived, and they had to return to Yarragon after an unfortunate set of circumstances resulted in most of their good potato crop being lost, placing them heavily in debt. Eugene was seven years younger than Charles and did not recall much about this event.

10 Charles remembered: "This episode took more out of Father than Eugene. As he watched the doctor operate on Eugene's nose, it was too much...and he suddenly fainted. The doctor had to stop...and attend to Father, who fortunately soon recovered."

11 An older north-western suburb of Melbourne.

12 Australian colloquialism often used by Eugene and meaning to be utterly sincere about something and to act on it.

13 Eugene was in his seventies at the time of our interviews. Some years after this, he abandoned the hairpiece in favour of his bald pate, as later photographs show.

III

For us to dare to live a life in which we continue to move out of the static places and take trusting steps in new directions – that is what faith is all about.

Henri Nouwen, *Intimacy, Fecundity and Ecstasy*[1]

Our desire for God is the desire that should govern all other desires.

Henri Nouwen, *Bread for the Journey*[2]

Rippling through my years: a life of faith and prayer

And Jesus said unto them, Come ye after me, and I will make you to become fishers of men. And straightway they forsook their nets and followed him.

Mark 1:17–18 KJV

So I was catapulted into adult life. I took to the roads in the battered Austin 7 with my newly gained driver's licence, wondering what would unfold. Summoning my courage, I sought an interview with Scott Brothers, who agreed to subcontract me as a courier, doing deliveries and acting as a taxi for my boss when he needed to visit a client somewhere in the city. Eventually, I began working for one or two other places, and my little business gradually grew. As I sought to land on my feet, the continued support of the Armadale Baptist Church provided a welcome stability.

By 1938, when I was twenty-three, Australia, along with the rest of the world, was shakily emerging from the Great Depression years and the devastating aftermath of the First World War. Personally, nationally and internationally, people were rebuilding their lives. Yet there were long shadows, and in September 1939, in a desperate attempt to halt German aggression, Britain declared war on Germany. Within hours, Australia and several other countries declared war in support of Britain, plunging us into another World War.

Kew Baptist Church in 1923 - courtesy of Kew Baptist Church

During this time of widespread upheaval, I joined the Baptist church in Kew[3], an eastern suburb of Melbourne. This proved to be another major turning point in my life, and the people there helped me greatly during the traumatic years of transition and beyond into my adult life. The church was a very vibrant place, with many gifted leaders and a marvellous group of young people, who welcomed me warmly and helped me come out of my shell. There was a buoyancy about this community in spite of the ever-present sufferings of the war years, and the horizons of my life expanded dramatically. Multifaceted avenues of learning, service and leadership opened for me, and I was nourished continually by the life of worship and prayer. Slowly, a tentative self-confidence began to emerge in me.

Looking back over fifty years living with this church, I am vividly aware of how much this community of faith has enriched me and helped to shape who I have become. That I have remained a member of this congregation for so long is a remarkable thing in itself. This has been the place from which I have gone out into all the other areas of my life—my family, the business, overseas travel, various forms of mission and evangelism. From all of these, I have returned and gone out again in a familiar rhythm that has blessed and sustained me. Ruth and I were married here, our children were dedicated, baptised and married here. Ruth's funeral was held here,[4] as well as the funerals of other relatives and dear friends. I expect my own will happen here, too. A great deal of my living is held in this place and among these people.

* * *

Kew Baptist had one of the largest Christian Endeavour Societies in the state. This was an international, interdenominational movement designed to train young people in discipleship, both in theory and practice.[5] I quickly became very involved in the Young People's Department. Everyone participated in the worship, prayer, and study activities and then also selected one area of practical service. Since I was already passionate about evangelism,[6] I joined the evangelism committee and became its convenor for many years. It was such a gift to be able to work with other young people who had the same calling. I also held the position of Vice President of the Christian Endeavour Society for some time, and these leadership roles helped to build my confidence, which had been so badly eroded during the trauma of my teens and early adult years. I learned that I was a good organiser and administrator, something I had begun to notice in running my small business. These two areas of my life worked together, re-enforcing my gifts and helping to build my fragile self-esteem in positive ways.

At that time, we had so many young people wanting to be involved in evangelism that we were able to move beyond our local church to teach Sunday school and preach at other churches in the industrial suburbs of Melbourne and throughout rural Victoria. I organized the preaching and teaching teams of young people in order to respond to the requests that inundated us during these fruitful years of service.

On one visit somewhere in the Warrnambool area,[7] which was quite a distance, our team arrived at the church in good time for the service, which I was to lead. Our preacher was the leader of the Young People's Department, and everyone looked up to him. About one minute before we were due to start, he said to me: "Eugene, I don't have a message yet. Nothing has come to me, so I'll just go outside and take a walk around the church and in due course I know I'll get the message. You start the service, but keep it going for a while until I come back." I had little choice but to go into the pulpit and begin the service. We moved, as gradually as I could manage, through the prayers, hymns, readings and offering. All the time, I wondered what I would do if he didn't come back in time for the sermon! Just at the moment when he was needed, the young preacher returned with a broad smile on his face. As he passed me on his way into the pulpit, he whispered: "Eugene, I've got it! I've got it!" He went on to preach quite a good sermon, to my very great relief. He was an individualist and broke all the rules of everything, but he was a very effective soul-winner and was used by the Lord to build others up in their faith.

I was not one of the preachers in these evangelistic endeavours, because my stammer made me hesitant about any public speaking. But I was often asked to give my testimony, and this stretched my shaky confidence to its limits. One Sunday, not long after the war had started, we were invited to Sale[8] Baptist Church for an evangelistic service. The whole team piled into the back of my van, as we usually did, and off we went. It was suggested that I give my testimony that evening, but since my stammer was still a serious problem, I wasn't very keen about doing this. However, some pressure was put on me and I reluctantly agreed. When the time came for me to speak, I went forward with a good deal of trepidation, but to my great surprise, the Lord gave me unexpected liberty of speech. Apparently, my words had some influence on the congregation, particularly several young nurses from the nearby hospital. But I only know this because about four or five years ago, one of those nurses was passing through Melbourne, and she arranged to meet up with the young preacher from our group, by now considerably advanced in years. While they were reminiscing, she asked about me and told him that my testimony had helped her and several of her friends become Christians.

Fifty years later, I had the immense surprise and joy of hearing what happened that night! I was quite overwhelmed and felt humbled and grateful to the Lord for his help and for this woman's faithfulness over the years. Her generosity of spirit in referring to my testimony after such a long time was a surprising gift to me. It was really staggering, because I clearly remember how afraid I was of speaking that night and how sure I was that my words would be extremely inadequate and not of much benefit to anyone. It is a delight to remember again that the Lord frequently uses the weak to do surprising things. Throughout my life, I've learned how we are often unaware of the way we may have been used by the Lord to help someone else. But as we get older, we sometimes get to hear such lovely things, and they are gentle blessings from the Lord, encouragements about how we have lived as disciples in our ordinary lives. I'm very grateful for these unexpected moments.

At Westgarth Baptist,[9] on a similar occasion, there were seven conversions, and I've kept in touch with one of the men, who has gone on in his faith and become an elder in his church. There were many other such moments and we endeavoured to support all these people in their new faith, helping them to find a church community where they would be nurtured. It was a considerable challenge because there were quite a lot of them, and it is very encouraging to still hear from some of them like this.

Every Friday night, I organised another regular preaching commitment at an open-air meeting in Kew around the corner from the church in Glenferrie Road near Liddiard Street. Because it was Friday night, there were crowds of people, and some would stop and listen to the music, testimonies and preaching. At the time, I played cornet in the band, and one evening, as we started up enthusiastically, I played a wrong note loudly enough for it to be heard very clearly by everyone, and all the people burst into spontaneous laughter. It was excruciating for me, and I never played again. I can still feel how ashamed and mortified I was. But I appreciate greatly the deepening of my faith and prayer during this period of my life and the wise guidance we received from the pastors and others in the church.[10]

* * *

Within the Young People's Christian Endeavour Society, I found a place where I could actively pursue my study of the Bible, theology and other areas of interest. I also learned to lead worship, pray in public and present papers. In spite of my terrible stammer and lack of confidence, I appreciated the opportunity to research and write papers and to present them to an audience of peers for discussion and review, as I was always painfully aware of my lack of formal education. Over time, my confidence improved, and within this group I discovered a diverse group of friends with whom I could share my faith—including Ruth, who eventually became my wife.

I became very interested in doctrine and practical theology—how I could live out my faith in my ordinary, everyday life. I did not always agree with the views of the people I was reading, but I do recall very clearly how much the writings impacted my life, both challenging me and clarifying my insights into my own life of faith and prayer.

I was very eager to learn about the practical living of the holy and sanctified life, both from Scripture and in church history. I found many divergent opinions about the experience of sanctification[11]—from Keswick to Finney to Hudson Taylor to Wesley. But the view that appealed to me most was that when we become Christian, we mean business with the Lord and are united to Christ. Though Christ becomes pre-eminent in our lives, we still retain our individuality and free will. We are not completely dominated, and our personalities are not wiped out, but we are one with Christ in our own uniqueness. I liked that.

Wesley put a lot of emphasis on the importance of "entire sanctification," or the second work of grace, which as I understand it is the core desire to love God and other people, and this brings a conscious awareness at all times of God's abiding presence. I've never felt I should go along with one viewpoint or another as if it were everything, but I do believe that the inner desire to love God and others wholly is of central importance, and this has been my core prayer since I was young. Of course, it is taking all my life to develop this love in me, but by the grace of God and my cooperation with that grace, I am moving in the right direction, I hope. Essentially, I believe that this is the process of sanctification in me.

In general, I think that people in the church today seem less interested in the rich meaning of sanctification than they were fifty years ago. I think if you asked most of them what it means they would not know what you were talking about. This worries me a little. Even though young people are on the whole better educated today, and there are aspects of the Christian life which are perhaps better now than back then, there seems to be a lack of theological depth, a lack of concern with some of the deeper truths. I think the overall challenge of what it means to be a Christian was clearer in those days.

Of course, things used to be much more black and white then. We didn't go to the pictures, or dance, or drink alcohol, or anything like that. Things were either sinful, or not, and the groups I was in accepted these boundaries and had plenty of other interests. Clearly, this was a very narrow, legalistic view of acceptable Christian behaviour, and many things have changed for the better. But sometimes I think we've gone too far in the other direction, so that now almost anything is alright. That's not good either. As always, the challenge is to be more balanced.

In the past, people went to ministers with the concerns of their lives, but now they go to psychologists or counsellors. I know that these professions have very helpful insights into the working of the human mind and psyche, but I am uneasy because we are forgetting the wisdom and power of the Holy Spirit. More than we realise, I think that the church today places less emphasis on the lifelong work of the Holy Spirit in us, the process of transformation and the importance of our being open to the life of God growing in us and our part in cooperating with that process.

* * *

During those early years at Kew, I was also drawn into a life of deeper discipleship and transformation through the Fisherman's Club, which was started and led by the young preacher I mentioned above. This group was for young men with a concern for evangelism, and the name came from the Gospel story of Jesus telling his first disciples, who were fishermen, that if they followed him he would make them fishers of men.[12] We met at eight o'clock every Sunday morning to study the Bible and discuss how to follow Jesus more closely and also to pray for one another and the various activities of the church. Our time together was rich in fellowship, and it nurtured and strengthened the foundations of our faith as we learned to pray together deeply. The memories of those times have continued to unfold through my whole life, and I'm very moved when I recall the gift that group has proved to be to me.

During one of these meetings, although the focus of our gathering and discussion had nothing at all to do with my business, as I left the meeting room I had the distinct impression that the Lord was asking me to expand my fledgling business. This came as a very great surprise, something of a shock, as at the time I was very determined not to allow the business to take over the central focus of my life, which was my relationship with the Lord and my commitment to evangelism. At first, I completely dismissed this call, but it was persistent. Even so, it was some time before I decided that it was genuine. I have often pondered the mystery of how this life-changing call came sideways to me through this club of young men. In my conscious awareness, my intention was to go in the exact opposite direction by *not* expanding the business. Looking back, I see now that the expansion of the business was not unrelated to my love of the Lord and my commitment to evangelism, but rather through God's goodness and help, the business eventually enabled me to engage in and support evangelism throughout the world, far beyond the horizons of my world on that ordinary Sunday morning at Kew Baptist Church.

Nowadays, I think of evangelism in a very wide, broad way. I believe that it must be concerned with the total welfare of people—not just their souls. Thus, if people are hungry or destitute, preaching the Gospel and proclaiming the Kingdom of God includes finding ways to help them move out of this. This is very clear in Scripture.[13] Today, I love to search out the cutting edges of evangelism, and it has been a joy to be able to support so many ministries through Mission Enterprises. This experience reveals to me how much God longs to give us—so much more than we can even begin to imagine.[14]

This widening stream of discipleship developed its flow from smaller interests when I was quite young. From the time of my seventeen-year-old decision to trust God's Word, I was interested in reading about how to allow the life of God within me to develop (sanctification); how to share my faith (evangelism); how to savour the joy of learning about significant movements of God around the world (revivals); and how to support fullness of life in people (healing). I see now that these different interests are all connected, and I am amazed at how God has led me to where I am now as an old man, still engaging actively, with both intense pleasure and struggle in each area.

My years at Kew Baptist provided avenues where these interests were deepened by study and experience, leading me out into larger ministries that have continued to shape my life. My youthful endeavours were extended by my election to the diaconate in 1949 when I was thirty-four,[15] which brought me into leadership within the wider church community in a number of ways, one being my help with the church's local evangelistic crusades (which most Baptist churches around the world conducted at that time). My contribution to these events was mostly through administration and counselling, and these experiences granted me wisdom that has helped me in later years.

* * *

My studies with the Young People's group provided a context in which to develop my interest in the history of revivals around the world, and I enthusiastically researched the extraordinary phenomenon of the outpouring of God's Spirit on particular churches and regions throughout history. This outpouring often spearheaded movements for social change, such as the abolition of slavery, prison reforms, and the push for universal education. The thought of such widespread transformation thrilled my soul. I read everything I could get my hands on about John Wesley, George Whitfield, Charles Finney, Martin Luther, John Calvin, and other old-time evangelists and teachers in America, England and Europe. I loved reading about times and places when God seemed to be doing a new thing. This strong attraction to the history and experience of revival, and my deep yearning to experience it in our own time, is connected with my life-long call and passion for evangelism.

When I was in my late thirties/early forties, I became very active with the Youth for Christ ministry in Melbourne, which at that time was relatively new. An international, interdenominational movement, it focused on bringing young people to Christ and nurturing their faith. This movement began in America in the 1940s and rapidly spread around the world. When young people responded to a call for commitment to Jesus Christ at any of the evangelistic rallies, they were each assigned a counsellor, who was responsible for talking with them and keeping in touch until they were grounded in a community of faith. For many years, I was an advisor, whose role was to support the male counsellors at our rallies and help them connect the converts with appropriate communities of faith. I loved the emphasis in this movement on calling young people to follow the way of Jesus and supporting them as they matured in faith, and I particularly appreciated the emphasis on reaching those who were unchurched as well. I spent some years as a board member and also chairman and committed regular financial support to the organisation which I still do.

Australia Youth for Christ Ministry Service Award presented to Eugene - courtesy of the Veith family

In 1959, my commitment to evangelism was further stretched through my participation in the first Billy Graham Crusade in Australia. The dynamic American Baptist minister had a growing world-wide ministry, and his fifteen-week crusade in Australia was awaited eagerly by some and uneasily by others. The organisation of the events was meticulous. Thousands of prayer meetings were held around the country and hundreds of people were trained as counsellors and advisors. I was invited to be an advisor. In Melbourne alone, around 719,000 people attended twenty-five meetings, the largest being on 14 March at the Melbourne Cricket Ground, which drew 143,750 people, a record for a single venue and for the famous site.[16] At that time, I was in my mid-forties and had been a member of the diaconate in our church for ten years. We supported the crusade, and I was invited to be part of the support team for people who responded to Billy Graham's altar call at the end of each meeting. I was deeply moved as I repeatedly watched hundreds of people quietly leave their seats and move slowly to stand in front of the central platform.

Choir at one Billy Graham meeting at the Myer Music Bowl Melbourne 1959
- courtesy of the Veith family

After Billy Graham had prayed for these people, he told them there was a counsellor beside them who would pray with them and hear their longings and help them understand the first practical steps of faith. When this was done, the counsellors brought each person to their assigned adviser, who ensured that the person making a commitment to Christ was comfortable with the care they had received and had ongoing church support in place. As one of the advisors each evening, I found this a very moving experience. Throughout Australia, I continue to meet people who were converted at one of those meetings and still regard it as a watershed in their lives. Though there were sceptics, for me this was a time of great joy in watching the healing and transforming life of God work in astounding ways with hundreds, sometimes thousands, of people. I will never forget the experience or the privilege it was to be a part of it. I feel that in many ways it was the closest thing to revival we have experienced in this country.

Of course, revivals can also bring a shadow side and the need for discernment and a period of testing for the fruits of the Spirit—just as in biblical times.[17] But while I know that there are often problematic aspects associated with them, I feel that the testimony of church history indicates that there *are* unexpected and authentic times of real revival. For years I have longed and prayed for spiritual revival to come to our land and to other places, especially my beloved France. I have a great love for that country and culture because of my French heritage, and I have prayed regularly for the French people to be blessed with spiritual well-being. I've visited several times and would love to visit there again before I die.

I am always keen to hear about contemporary revivals in other places and still spend several hours a day reading journals about these movements of God in our time. My desire is not only to be aware of them as historical events, but to learn from them in practical ways for the ordinary living of my life, because they enable me to recognise and understand something about the present-day movements of God around the world. Sometimes I have been fortunate enough to know someone who has been living in a place where revival has broken out, and I love to hear firsthand the stories and impressions of how God is transforming people and the world.

In my own journey of transformation, I have found that the most clarity has come from meditating on the Word of God and sitting quietly in God's presence every day. The hours I spend meditating on the Word of God are very enriching, illuminating and life changing, as that time helps me both to appreciate and to question everything that I am reading, living and pondering. My daily practice of sitting in God's presence helps me to see ways of actually living what I am learning, and this has become a way of discerning what is important and what is not. Of course, I don't mean that I am perfect in any of this! Even now, I am still on the journey of growing into all of these things. I am more aware than ever of how much I just don't know.

As I pay attention to what is growing in me, I am realising how many of the seeds sown in me during childhood and adolescence have been nourished, protected, encouraged and carried forward into maturity and fruition by the Spirit of God amongst the people of the Kew Baptist Church. I recall with immense gratitude wonderful preachers, mentors and friends. The community is not without its quirks and difficulties, of course, but my fellowship here has been one of the most formative aspects of my life for over half a century and it is the place where I found my wife and where my children and grandchildren have been welcomed and nurtured in faith.

Endnotes

1 Nouwen, Henri, *Intimacy, Fecundity and Ecstasy*, cited in *The Only Necessary Thing: Living a prayerful Life* Compiled and edited by Wendy Wilson Greer, Great Britain, Darton, Longman and Todd Ltd. 2000, p. 194

2 Nouwen, Henri, cited in *The Only Necessary Thing: Living a Prayerful Life.* Compiled and edited by Wendy Greer Wilson. Great Britain, Darton, Longman and Todd Ltd. 2000, 194, 27.

3 Kew Baptist church was established in 1856 making it one of the oldest Baptist churches in the State of Victoria

4 Ruth died in 1989, the same year I recorded Eugene's life story. He lived another twenty-one years after this. After his death and private funeral in 2010, the Thanksgiving Service for his life was held in the Kew Baptist Church, bringing to completion his seventy-year association with this fellowship.

5 At this time there were three Departments—Junior, Intermediate and Young People and a total of around 170 members. Eugene's involvement was with the Young People's Department. The Society celebrated its Golden Jubilee in 1940 and some of its vibrancy is captured in the history it produced in that year. "No Depression Here!" the history stated. The 1943 report notes that twenty-nine

members of the Young Peoples Department were absent on "active service for King and Country," while those at home took great pains to remain in touch with them through a much-appreciated monthly communiqué. Jill L. Manton, *A History of the Kew Baptist Church 1856–1981: the first one hundred and fifty years.*

6 Evangelism refers to the proclamation of the Gospel in various contexts for the purpose of calling people to commit themselves to Christ and encourage them in active discipleship.

7 Large coastal city in western Victoria.

8 Large country town in eastern Victoria.

9 Inner northern suburb of Melbourne.

10 Pastors of Kew Baptist Church during Eugene's formative years in the YPSCE, who were each very significant in his early faith development: Rev J.E. Newnham (1926–1941); Rev L.J. Gomm (1944–1952); Dr F.W. Boreham Acting minister during war years (1941–1944) while Mr Gomm was an army chaplain; Mr Newnham remained on as President of the YPSCE during the interim pastorate of the war years whilst undertaking his new role as Victorian Home Mission Superintendent.

11 Term meaning the gradual transformation in a person through an intentional attending to the presence of the Spirit of God within them and allowing the changes this brought. There were many different views on this as Eugene states, but he gives his own understanding here which is the core of his life.

12 Matthew 4:18–19.

13 James 2:14–17.

14 Ephesians 3:20.

15 In a Baptist church the diaconate is a lay leadership group elected by the congregation to support and work with the pastor/s in all areas of church life. Eugene served as a deacon for several decades and was highly respected in the church community.

16 See Billy Graham Crusade www. emelbourne.net.au/biogs, published by School of Historical Studies, Department of History, The University of Melbourne. Also the Melbourne Cricket Ground site giving a summary of the biggest attendance states: "Ironically it is not a sporting event which holds the attendance record at the MCG. This honour belongs to American evangelist Billy Graham who in 1959 attracted an estimated crowd of 130,000 (some estimates go as high as 143,750) many of whom had spilled over onto the arena." www.mcg.org.au/history/attendance

17 See the exhortation to test the spirits and the fruits of the experience to see if they resonate with the Spirit of God as revealed in Jesus, in 1 John 4:1-3.

IV

A good marriage can best be described by four images:
A good marriage is a warm fireplace.
A good marriage is a big table loaded with lots of food and drink.
A good marriage is a container that holds suffering.
A good marriage is Christ's body, flesh that is "food for the world."

–Ronald Rolheiser, *Against an Infinite Horizon* [1]

The crucible of daily living

Beloved, let us love one another; for love is of God, and everyone who loveth is born of God and knoweth God.

–1 John 4:7 KJV

Ruth Wilson was one of the many young people in the Christian Endeavour Society at Kew Baptist Church, and we were attracted to each other soon after I arrived. We went together for two or three years and were married in January 1942, when the Second World War was raging, and I was twenty-six years old. I was running a one-man business and could only afford to take the weekend off, so we married on the Saturday of the Australia Day long weekend and had Sunday and Monday for our honeymoon.

Eugene and Ruth - courtesy of the Veith family

We stayed in a guest house at Kilsyth in the beautiful Dandenong Ranges to the east of Melbourne, a popular area for holidays. On our return we lived for a time with Ruth's grandmother, Grace, in Kew, but soon moved to our own place in Wills Street, Kew. It had a lovely block of land—ninety feet at the front and one hundred and sixty feet at the back, with lots of trees and an old house on it, expansive enough for our dreams. There was room to accommodate my small business and plenty of room for the family we were planning to have. We really enjoyed it.

Ruth loved children dearly, and so she was delighted when ours began to arrive: first David, who was followed by Anne, then John and after a gap of some years, Adele. We felt very blessed to have two boys and two girls. But even though they shared the same parents and upbringing, we soon noticed how very different they were. We found that it was important to treat each one individually—not in the sense of favouring them one above the other, but in the way we related to each of them as unique people with different personalities and approaches to life.

We also quickly realised how different we were from each other—totally different, except perhaps in our mutual love of the Lord, each other and our children. Our complete commitment to the welfare of each other and our family and the sincere desire to follow the way of the Lord in all aspects of our life together was the glue which held us fast through ordinary and tumultuous times.

Over the years, we both struggled to live with our differences, because they permeated everything. Ruth was sensitive and very devoted to me and the children. I used to tell her sometimes, "Ruth you love me too much!" and she would laugh. But she was very conservative and cautious. Learning to put up with a funny bloke like me must often have tried her patience. My expansiveness, new ideas and initiative in making things happen often scared the wits out of her. We had to compromise continually and learn from each other, but in spite of goodwill and perseverance, neither of us changed in our essential nature. We discovered this basic difference was a reality we could not resolve. Perhaps I changed a little, in that I realised that her cautious conservatism was sometimes good for me, but I doubt that Ruth felt my wide ideas and eagerness to explore new possibilities made her more venturesome. Nevertheless, she did accept me as I was, and I accepted her as she was, although this sincere resolve of ours proved to be a continual challenge. It came up all the time and we had to keep dealing with it on a daily basis. I think sometimes, especially in the early days, we each hoped we might change the other a bit, but on the whole, we had to learn to cope with the fact that we both remained essentially the same, and we tried to give each other the necessary space to be ourselves. This is the challenge of marriage.

I suppose, being really truthful, we never actually agreed fully about anything! In matters concerning how the household was managed and run, even if I thought some things were unnecessary, I'd defer to Ruth's wishes and judgement. But in matters involving our parenting, we often had to compromise. One basic difference between us was expressed in our different attitudes to discipline with our children. Ruth tended to be stricter than me and to get more upset about some things than I thought was necessary. Concerning pocket money, she might have wanted to give them ten cents and I wanted to give twenty cents, so we compromised with fifteen cents. She was always a very loving and caring mother, but I felt she worried about the children too much, and she thought I didn't worry enough. When they were older and out with friends on Saturday night, she was very anxious if they were later than our midnight curfew in coming home. She could never go to sleep until they were all safely back under the family roof. I could go off to sleep anytime. Maybe that was partly because I knew she would keep awake, but I think it was mostly because we were different.

We had disagreements about money, about the best way to deal with the children as they went through the different phases of growing up, about the wisest thing to do in a whole variety of circumstances. Sometimes Ruth and I agonised over these things, but we never allowed anything to become such a problem that it upset the whole household or threatened to destroy our marriage and family. On the whole, we made a good combination in the training of our children because we balanced one another.

We also had enormous difficulties with time. I liked to arrive at the church an hour or so early when I had some responsibilities as a deacon on Sundays. Ruth, who didn't drive, needed to come with me. But in spite of all the years of my saying we had to leave on time, Ruth was seldom ready and I was always late. I found this annoying and she thought I was too fussy about the matter. These relatively small things remained a constant challenge for us!

When Ruth and I did not agree and had to make a decision, I felt that as the husband and head of the household, I needed to take on this responsibility. Ruth agreed with this scriptural principle, but I know it has been used wrongly to bring much injustice and sorrow into some homes. I do not think that it means the husband is the big boss in the family and should make decisions without regard to the feelings or wishes of his wife and children, for I believe very much in mutual discussion and deferring to one another in love. We are responsible to the Lord for doing so and for seeking the wellbeing of one another. But sometimes on matters of principle, when we can't agree, someone has to have the final responsibility, and I think then the husband must accept this as head of the family.[2] In society generally, someone has to take final responsibility for decisions or otherwise nothing would ever be accomplished, a reality that was underlined for me daily in my business life.

But in this as in all things, I realized that it was important that I be teachable and open to new light that might be cast on a subject, willing to change my behaviour with the humility and sensitivity that only the Lord can give. I always asked the Lord for the wisdom and grace to be teachable when I was wrong, and through this I was taught that I needed to compromise and bend, even if I thought my way still seemed the best. When we had differences and I was sure I was right, I would reflect on it in the Lord's presence, and the Lord often opened my mind and gave me a new perspective. I frequently realised that what Ruth said had some truth and wisdom in it, which I hadn't seen. Then I went back to her and said, "Well, I see what you're driving at, although I don't fully agree with you, but I do see there's a need for me to change my opinion."

But it's also true that I'm a person who hates arguments, and there was a temptation for me to give in on some things just for the sake of peace, relegating my responsibility on the matter. It was something I had to consider, because I knew my weakness in this regard, and I needed the grace of the Lord to teach me wisdom in this, too.

Sometimes, after a disagreement, I went back and said, "Ruth, I'm sorry I upset you"—even when I didn't know whether I had done the right thing, or not. I just knew it was important to say I'm sorry, because it was true and it would restore our relationship. I sought the Lord's guidance on all these matters and I am sure Ruth did the same. We discovered that our problems helped us to grow spiritually because we had to rely on the Lord's love and grace, and we learned to listen to each other more thoughtfully and apologise when we fell out with each other. Such testing[3] helped us appreciate each other and try to understand each other's viewpoint.

I was going to say it's a minor miracle that our marriage survived our differences, but I think it would be truer to say that it's a big miracle. The love of God, the grace of God, the goodness and blessings of the Lord enabled us to share a good life together and to bring up a lovely family. It was fascinating watching our children's lives unfold—and I am still enjoying seeing them unfold now in their adult lives.

Our first child, David, was a very lively and good natured kid, with bright red hair inherited from his maternal grandmother. He was rowdy, exuberant and generous in spirit, loved sport and getting up to all sorts of tricks. He was followed by Anne, who was a feisty, interesting, thoughtful little girl. From an early age she kept a diary in which she recorded some of her thoughts and observations. John arrived next. He was a very shy, sensitive child who felt things deeply. Like his brother, he also loved sport and getting up to tricks. Our large garden had lots of space at the side, where we played football and cricket most days. Even though I was very busy and had to work each night on the business books, I made it a regular practice to play with John and David until I was into my fifties. It was great fun and healthy and good for our relationship. Adele's birth ten years after John brought our family to completion. Because her siblings were all quite a bit older, her arrival brought a completely new dimension into the family, which was challenging and good for all of us. She too was red haired and very sensitive, but she had her own mind on most things. Perhaps we had learned more as parents by this time, too, for it seemed that we did not have to discipline her very much at all.

Eugene and Ruth with David, John, Anne and Adele (inset) - courtesy of the Veith family

Each of the children made personal decisions to commit their lives to Christ in their early teens, a fact which brought Ruth and me great joy. All of them have continued to develop and mature in their faith as adults and to find different avenues of service in the church and the world, which is very pleasing. Now our children are all married, and we have twelve grandchildren, some of whom have also made commitments to follow the Lord.

From the beginning, in spite of our differences, Ruth and I very intentionally tried to cultivate love in our home. We always had a particular empathy and fondness one for another. I remember David and John being real cobbers[4] and can't remember them ever fighting badly. We never had any real fights in the family, and there has hardly been anything said of a nasty nature. My mother was very gentle, and I think that has come through in our family. I find it very moving to recall her gentleness and to notice it more clearly now in my own family as well and I am very grateful for this.

We had family worship, reading and prayer together every night. I know that some families have tried this and it hasn't worked out, but I give thanks to the Lord that we never had any negative reaction from the children about it. I am sure that our children learnt more about the Lord at home than they did from church and Sunday School, because they saw God answering our prayers for ourselves as well as others. Even when the other children from the street were playing at our place or were here for the evening meal, we had our family worship, and they seemed to enjoy the time. I've always hoped that they benefited from it some way in their lives. We taught our children to love us and each other, as well as other people, but always to love God the most. We also taught them that God loved them and was their friend, and this sowed seeds in their lives which have brought forth much fruit.

I believe that parents are the most important way that children begin to know something about God, because they model what God is like for the child—for good and ill. Compassion and tenderness, forgiveness and reconciliation, justice and mercy, repentance and hope lived out in simple practical ways help to ground what it means to follow the way of Jesus. Children need to know for a fact that they are deeply loved by their parents, that their parents are truly interested in them and that they see each other and their children as gifts from God, for whom they are responsible.

Ruth and Eugene in the garden of their home in Wills Street, Kew - courtesy of the Veith family

But it is also true that there's only so much that even the best parents in the world can do. Children are individuals, and they will make their own choices as they grow up. But parents can do a lot by trusting their children to the Lord and not only teaching in words, but also in deeds about the love of God and how that looks in human life as Jesus has shown us. It is no use having family worship morning, noon and night and teaching children about God and the way of Jesus unless the children see this reflected in the lives of their parents and in the nitty gritty day to day life of their family. It's harder to live the Christian way of life at home than anywhere else, because you have to live it all of the time—and you're living it in a set of relationships that test you in the deepest places because they are so intimate.

It is important for children to see their parents relating to each other in loving ways and for the children to be treated justly and fairly, not favouring one more than the other. This includes how we as parents talk to one another and to our children. Children notice everything their parents do and say, either consciously or unconsciously, and they are quick to detect any marked discrepancy between what is said and what is done. We are told in Scripture to be courteous to all people, so how important it is to live this way at home, with humility, love and gentle firmness. This will then be consistent with all our dealings with people outside the family, where these same qualities need to be present. We can all express the qualities of Christ in the general tone and spirit of our ordinary conversation and in all the thousands of ordinary things we do: opening a door for a lady, being polite, listening to each other fairly—this kind of thing.

At times, I have been appalled by how some Christian parents relate to their children. Some spoil their children foolishly and others are so severe that the children are always in trouble. As in everything, balance seems to be really important. I think it is necessary to give children the space to express themselves, so it's important to give them the leeway to do this. A little rebelliousness can be a very good thing. It's bad to overprotect children or to dominate them and prevent them from being themselves.

Of course, it is important to take good care of them by making the home a safe place and ensuring that they are not put in situations that are beyond their years to manage. But at the same time, I believe it is very important not to make things too easy for them. They need to have skills for coping with the hard things in life, and so parents need to help them develop a healthy resilience to challenges. For this reason, I have real reservations about Christian schools, although I know there are good arguments both ways. But as parents, we have to prepare our children to go out into the world and cope. They need to know how to meet temptations, criticism and alternative world views to faith.

Parenting is very demanding. Most of us don't have any real training in the art of parenting, and so we stumble along. It's a learning process, and we need a lot of wisdom as well as patience and firm gentleness. In my parenting, I have found I need to stay close to the Lord, and so prayer has been essential. I pray for my children all the time. I have made this a daily commitment, and it has helped me be more aware of their struggles and needs.[5] When insurmountable problems arise and there don't seem to be any good answers, I have wrestled in prayer and fasted on behalf of my children. Prayer is the basis of it all, I think, as it is in everything.

Whatever I am doing, I am habitually aware of God's presence, so that I am not always consciously praying, but attending to the heartbeat of God that is within and behind everything. As I am wandering down the street, or driving in the car, or sitting in the office considering all sorts of problems related to running the business, I am in a prayerful mood, holding all before the Lord, open to his direction and guidance. This is how I am with my family too. They are always with me. The Lord sees my heart and knows me and is with me in everything—and my family is a big part of that.[6]

Of course, all sorts of things interrupt this. If I get out of bed in the morning and I'm in a bad mood or something really upsets me, I can lose this prayerful awareness. But the Lord knows this and holds my moods and tiredness and the upsets that interfere with this awareness, and so as I turn to him I can quickly get back to that awareness again. The Lord knows how we are made. He remembers we are dust and has compassion on us and helps us.[7] So these setbacks are also our teachers, and they can teach us a lot about ourselves and about God if we negotiate them with courage and faith.

* * *

In all these things, I have found that the Lord is very forgiving and gracious. Of course, it is also true that God is holy and our growth in holiness is really important. I don't think this is preached enough today, so I do not want to underrate that aspect of our walk with God. But I do believe that a lot of problems come from not accepting the Lord's forgiveness. Many of my problems in life have been because I haven't forgiven myself, and somehow the Lord has shown me that. He's given me such a deep sense of his forgiveness, and I'm ashamed that I haven't recognised that. I'm ashamed that the Lord has been so ready to forgive, but I haven't accepted it. I think a lot of people suffer from that. The Lord is more gracious and forgiving than we ever understand.

Of course, that's not to say he countenances sin. Some people may take this too lightly and say, "Oh, the Lord will forgive me. The Lord died for my sins. I'm forgiven." That is very careless. This is why repentance—being sorry and turning back to God—is so important. But repentance has become a real burden for some people, and this is sad, because it is an invitation to life rather than a threat or oppression. In family relationships, repentance—or saying sorry (and meaning it)—is one of the most important things in restoring and healing the things that have wounded or divided us. This is one of the greatest things parents can model for their children.

There is a passage in Zephaniah where the Lord says that he rejoices over us with gladness and singing.[8] Sometimes it is easier to experience such things than to describe them, and in this case, such an idea is staggering and beyond our finite minds to grasp. But to experience it in the heart! There, we are changed, and it is this relationship with God that I would like every young and old Christian to experience—the breadth, length, depth and height of the love of God.[9]

In marriage, we are invited to learn how to love God in daily life with our whole heart and mind and soul and strength and to love our neighbour as ourselves.[10] It is important for us to encourage one another to live out this essential commandment with the help of the Lord, because it is the central core of our faith. Though we may look to one another for support and encouragement, we must look to the Lord for our main source of inspiration and fulfilment. For while it is certainly a privilege to pray with and encourage one another and to minister to each other in all possible ways, in the final analysis, we each have to pursue our own deep relationship with him. I believe we should give each other the time and space to do that— and not crowd each other emotionally, but leave room for one another's creativity in reaching out for the Lord. Ruth and I tried to do this for each other, and it has been good.

The Lord has told us that we will live best when we love him first— before father, mother, spouse or children, before any other person, never mind how close we are to them and how much we love them. In fact, I have found that when we seek to love the Lord first, this increases our love for one another, for all people and the whole creation, far beyond the merely human world.

Endnotes

1 Rolheiser, Ronald. *Against an Infinite Horizon: The Finger of God in Our Everyday Lives*. New York: Crossroad, revised edition, 2001, 88-89. The fourth image of marriage invokes the Gospel understanding of Jesus the Christ: "And the Word became flesh and lived among us, and we have seen his glory, glory as of a father's only son, full of grace and truth" (John 1:14). This understanding was central to Eugene's faith and is the energy behind his desire to make his own love of God

"flesh" in the life of the world—especially in his family.

2 1 Corinthians 11:3; Ephesians 5:21-32.

3 1 Peter 1:6–7.

4 Australian colloquialism for mates, friends.

5 Most times when Eugene spoke of his intercessory prayers in general, he added a comment to the effect that praying for others made him more aware of their struggles and needs—as he does here in regard to his children. This was also a reason he encouraged his children to pray for others—to widen their awareness. See John V. Taylor, *The Go-Between God: The Holy Spirit and The Christian Mission* 1972; reprint, London: SCM Press Ltd., 1989, 232-233. He notes, "All true intercession is a deepening of awareness towards others rather than a request… when we realize [this] it brings a great change to our understanding of it. When praying for others we allow ourselves to be caught in the current of communication which the Spirit gives between us and another, and most of all between us and God." Such experience is very characteristic of Eugene's prayer.

6 Eugene frequently mentioned his habitual prayer underneath all his daily activities. The same phenomenon is mentioned by the Quaker Thomas Kelly (1893–1941) in *Reality of the Spiritual World* 1944; reprint, London: Quaker Home Service, 1996, 35-36. He writes: "The eternal prayer life…is carried on after one has left the quiet room, has opened the door and gone back into the noisy hubbub of the family group. It is carried on as one dashes for a trolley, as one lunches in a cafeteria, as one puts the children to bed. There is a way of living in prayer at the same time that one is busy with the outward affairs of daily living…The stabilizing of our lives, so that we live in God and in time, in fruitful interplay, is the task of maturing religious life" 35–36). Madame Guyon (1648–1717) observed this much earlier in *Experiencing the Depths of Jesus Christ*, vol. 2 of Library of Spiritual Classics: Auburn, Maine: Seed Sowers Christian Books, 67. She writes, "In the beginning you were led into His presence by prayer; but now, as prayer continues, the prayer actually becomes His presence. In fact, we can no longer say that it is prayer that continues. It is actually His presence that continues with you. This is beyond prayer."

7 Psalm 103:13–14.

8 Zephaniah 3:17.

9 Ephesians 3: 14–20.

10 Luke 10:25–28.

V

To have faith is to see everything against an infinite horizon....When we have the eyes of faith we see a certain divine glow shimmering within the ordinary, just as we see all that is ordinary against a horizon of the eternal.

–Ronald Rolheiser, *Against an Infinite Horizon*[1]

Meaning business with the Lord

For surely I know the plans I have for you, says the Lord, plans for your welfare and not for harm, to give you a future with hope.

–Jeremiah 29:11 NRSV

When I started the business working for Scott Brothers at the age of eighteen, I had one old vehicle—the Austin 7, all that was retrieved from the closing of the butcher's shop business. Later, I began delivering goods for other firms, and as the business slowly grew, I bought an Austin 10 van and then a Chevrolet van. For a while, my father joined me and was helpful in procuring several good customers, including the jewellers Hardy Bros. Ltd., but he soon moved on to other work. I was grateful for my small business, which was going along quite well. But I was extremely cautious about getting too involved because I did not feel that business ambitions were compatible with a serious life of faith.

On the Sunday morning, after the Fisherman's Club meeting where I received the surprising call to expand the business, I remember walking down the narrow path at the side of the church on the way to the worship service and saying to one of the other young men with me, "Somehow I feel the Lord wants me to expand the business and become a businessman." I was surprised about this because I had seen quite a number of people become sidetracked from their faith by worldly ambition, making their work or business into a god and I knew with certainty that this was not what I wanted with my life.

I wanted to mean business with the Lord, an apt phrase for a businessman and one which has been meaningful to me all of my adult life. For me, it means to be utterly serious about my relationship with the Lord and to follow his promptings in my life as sincerely and transparently as I know how to, because of the love I have for him. I wanted nothing to distract me from that. I wanted to put my energy into evangelism and other aspects of the Lord's work. As a consequence of this very clear inner stance, I did not plan to expand the business.

However, in spite of my initial resistance, the impression that the Lord had spoken to me remained very strong. I went to see my oldest brother, who was an accountant, and I spoke to others about it, but no one encouraged me to go forward. Nevertheless, because I continued to feel this persistent nudge of God, I decided to put into motion certain things that would help the business expand, even though I did not know the reason for it or where it would lead.

As I began to obey this call, I found that I knew instinctively how to run a business and that the basic business principles were really just common sense. During my teen years, when I was apprenticed to my father in the butchering business, I was painfully shy, stammered badly, was losing my hair and had little self-confidence—not a promising set of characteristics for the making of a successful businessman. But in spite of this I seemed to have a gift for business and even in those early days, I had an inner awareness that if only I had the opportunity, I would be a good businessman.

Apart from my apprenticeship, I've never worked for anyone else in my life. And yet I've always had the ability to know what is essential in a business deal and am not prone to get tied up with non-essentials. In everything—how I manage my business, my social life and my life of faith—I like to get down to the nitty gritty. This ability has held me in good stead in my walk with the Lord and my understanding of people.

So I went ahead a step at a time, and I gradually began to realise that it is possible to run a business efficiently and Christianly at the same time. I could be a good businessman as well as a man of deep faith. This was a revelation to me. Moreover, I have found that in many ways, this is a really helpful combination. I was naturally out there in the world, mixing with all sorts of people who had no association with the church. Through my business activities, I learned to relate to people of all walks of life whom I would not have met if I had stayed only within the faith community. This has enriched my life and experience immensely and made me much more confident about moving easily in secular society and speaking naturally of my faith in this context, whenever it is relevant.

For this reason, I think it is a mistake for young people to enter theological college straight from university or college and then go immediately into the pastoral ministry. They might find themselves in a greenhouse atmosphere where they never learn how to relate to people who are not involved in church life. That eventually becomes a problem both for the congregation and for the Gospel in the market place.

Eugene and his father packing the delivery van - courtesy of the Veith family

When I married Ruth the business operated from the back of our property in Wills Street. Because the house was situated on a large block, and there was a laneway running behind all the houses in the street, the trucks entered and left in that way causing little disturbance to our neighbours. There was room to park the vehicles when they were not in use and they could not be seen from the street, which made things more secure and did not intrude too much on our neighbours or family. My office was there too and a large shed for the storage of delivery items and other necessities. On one occasion the shed was robbed causing considerable drama in our lives, but in general it was an ideal location for the business. In addition, there were many advantages for the family in my being on site when the children were little. Ruth was not isolated as some young mothers are and the children came in and out of the office. I could see much more of them than if I were away from home all day. At night it was easy for me to work on the books in a corner of our living room where the family gathered in other activities. Our lives were well integrated in this way and the business grew consistently. After the war ended in 1945, it really began to flourish.

The van with the roller blinds - courtesy of the Veith family

Eventually, I started a private company called Veith Transport,[2] and by 1950 we had two trucks and a small van with smart roller blind signs naming the original stores for which we did exclusive deliveries: Dunklings, Prouds, Gaunts & Hardy Bros.[3] Like our Melbourne trams, we could change the signs according to our destination by scrolling the blinds appropriately. We enjoyed that. The business continued to grow until we had six trucks and we could not accommodate any more on the property. With some reluctance, we decided to sell our home in Wills Street. Though it had provided wonderful space for our growing family and the expanding business, the house was old and required a lot of maintenance, the foundations needed repair, and the land was now too small for both our family and the business. We had been very happy there, but we knew it was time to separate the family home and the business operation.

Around the end of 1960, our family moved to a new home on Harp Road in East Kew, and the business moved to Burwood Road in Hawthorn, a nearby suburb, where there was some spare land at the back of the Shell service station. The land was owned by Shell, but we were permitted to build a small place there for an office, and we had an agreement that we would use their petrol for our vehicles and pay them rent for the land. We continued to operate from this Hawthorn depot until 1980, expanding it significantly during the intervening years.[4]

For many years, we employed no sales persons except myself, and we had no advertising. This saved us a great deal of money and helped the business prosper. In our efforts to honour the Lord in all our dealings, we found that our company was respected in the industry, and our expansion grew from recommendations as clients passed the Veith name on to other people. When someone phoned for information about our services, I would visit them, and it was extraordinary how easy it was to get business, in spite of the highly competitive market we faced from other big transport companies, such as Mayne Nicholas and Yellow Express.

At the end of each day, I made it my practice to retire to my study and sit in the Lord's presence. I was always aware of how I had been helped in the ways I needed—the right person coming along at the right time, unexpected openings and solutions to problems which surprised me. Sitting in the quietness, I was moved repeatedly to tears of gratitude for the gracious, generous presence of the Lord, helping me and working in all aspects of the business in spite of my very human limitations.

* * *

In August 1960, as the business continued to expand, we formed another company called Mission Enterprises.[5] This was a major step of faith for me in the unfolding of the "impossible dream" I had received as a child. It was a deeply moving experience for Ruth as well, and I remember that we signed the papers at her bedside, where she was resting following the birth of our youngest child, Adele.

We had always given as much to the Lord's work as we could, but the whole philosophy of this new company was to make money that we could give away for the Lord's work—all of it. It had always been my intention to establish such a company, and it was wonderful to finally have the resources to do it. The new company started with four vehicles and had its own specific purpose, distinct from Veith Transport. In all, we now had ten trucks:

Eugene Veith - courtesy of the Veith family

six for Veith Transport and four for Mission Enterprises. We extended our space at Hawthorn by acquiring additional land close by for an office and the growing number of trucks. Although we did experiment with developing one or two other small businesses[6] within Mission Enterprises, we soon decided that the new company would also operate mainly within the transport industry, because we found that it was better to concentrate our efforts where we had the most experience. By the late sixties, the business had expanded to the extent that I could no longer continue managing sales as well as everything else.

In the early seventies, Dirk Bakker and Stuart Brown joined Ron Nethercott and I as company directors and senior management personnel. This made a tremendous difference to what we could do. Ron and Stuart managed the transport division of the business, while Dirk developed a range

Dirk Bakker - courtesy of Dirk Bakker

of ministries loosely termed "the XYZ division". They were a fabulous leadership team,[7] who were very committed to the ethos and vision of Mission Enterprises and met weekly for management meetings and prayer for all aspects of the business as well as agreeing to draw as little as possible in salaries in order that more could be given away. We worked well together and I greatly appreciated their

Stuart Brown - courtesy of the Veith family

different gifts and experience as well as their deep faith and generous spirits. We complemented each other and in this way we were able to achieve much more than would ever have been possible otherwise. Much of the expansion of the business was due to their hard work and faithfulness to our vision.

Ron Nethercott - courtesy of the Veith family

By 1974, Veith Transport and Mission Enterprises had grown beyond our wildest imaginings, and Ruth and I decided to hand over the forty-year-old private family business Veith Transport to the not-for-profit company Mission Enterprises.[8] To be able to do this was a great joy, the sort of thing we had been working towards all those years. After that, the business grew even faster. Because Mission Enterprise was a non-profit company, all the profits were given away, and we could conserve more capital to develop the business even further.

By 1980, the transport division of Mission Enterprises operated thirty-two trucks with thirty-two parcel runs[9] from a conglomerate of buildings and land in Hawthorn. After more than twenty years in that area, we moved again to accommodate the expanding business, and we settled on Franklyn Street in Huntingdale, one of the rapidly developing eastern suburbs of Melbourne. We were now handling a huge volume of parcels, with forty-eight parcel runs daily. The move to a larger facility enabled us to change the way the dock at the depot operated. In particular, the unique colour-coded floor-level steel conveyor belt allowed drivers on one side of the belt to pre-sort the parcels they had picked up during the day by unloading them onto specific colours. On the other side of the belt, dock staff unloaded each group of parcels into matching colour-coded bins, ready for reloading the trucks the following morning for the day's deliveries. This simple scheme greatly improved the overall efficiency of the dock.[10] But by the mid-1980s the site at Huntingdale was reaching capacity, with sixty sub-contractor trucks and their sixty daily parcel runs.

Huntingdale depot showing some of the parked trucks - courtesy of the Veith family

Trucks being unloaded onto the conveyor belt at the Huntingdale depot - courtesy off the Veith family

In addition to these there was a sub-contracted taxi fleet of various vehicle sizes, which started with ten and grew to sixty, and another fleet of twenty courier vehicles located in the north of the city. These courier and taxi vehicles did not come to the depot, but were in contact with it by radio, delivering parcels that had been left behind or were in the wrong truck. These vehicles helped to ensure that we always honoured our next-day delivery guarantee. They also made direct deliveries to clients who made bulk orders, as it was far simpler and less expensive to deliver these loads directly, without returning to the depot.

Once again, we were challenged by this rapid expansion of the business. In prayer, I wrestled with many decisions. Was it time to move again? To upgrade our facilities and equipment? Or were we being called to do something different? The board also prayed about these decisions, as there were positive options both ways. But the price of land was rising, and the operation was becoming more sophisticated, requiring new equipment that would have cost several million dollars. I was also nearing retirement, as were two of the other directors. Five years earlier, Mayne Nicholas[11] had approached us to buy Veith Transport and Mission Enterprises, but we had withdrawn from the idea. Now we wondered about re-opening the possibility, and we eventually negotiated the sale in 1986.

At Mayne Nicholas's request, the existing staff and directors continued on through the transition period,[12] and they kept the Veith name. They agreed to develop a larger depot site in the adjoining suburb of Clayton, which opened in 1988—the most modern and well-equipped site of its kind in Australia, nearly twice the size of Huntingdale, operating over one hundred trucks under the name Veith Parceline.

The new owners kept on our manager, along with some of the office staff, so there is still a Christian influence in the place, and whenever I visit I am welcomed very warmly. After the sale the Mission Enterprises name was retained by us and became an investment company that continues to distribute the majority of its income to mission activity in Australia and around the world.[13]

I forget how many vehicles I had when I received the unexpected call to expand the business—probably two or three—but eventually we had over 180 drivers operating the blue trucks with the Veith name. They became a very familiar sight on the streets of Melbourne and its suburbs. At one time, our office, dock and Mission Enterprise staff numbered three hundred, and when we sold in 1986, we were the largest capital city metro parcel organisation in Australia, with a capacity of approximately 25,000 parcels per day. Even though my intention in the business had always been to give away as much as possible, I had no idea that the Lord would be so good to us or that it would grow to such an extent. I am still amazed at how everything worked out.

One of the later Veith trucks
- courtesy of the Veith family

Of course, over the more than fifty years before we sold the large and rapidly expanding businesses, we had experienced many daunting challenges and innumerable obstacles. The transport business is inherently very tough with a small margin for profit, requiring very careful management if it is to survive. I began the business during the Great Depression, and those difficult years were followed by the trauma of the Second World War. But through all these tough economic times, I was very conscious of the Lord's presence helping me, giving me wisdom and courage and meeting me in unexpected and practical surprises that consolidated the business and helped it to flourish.

At times we had problems with different people on the staff— the clash of personalities, different working habits or styles, varying abilities. As the business expanded, there were many people to supervise—hundreds of them at times—but we tried to keep a harmonious work environment and to ensure the welfare of each person. On the whole, I dealt with all the personnel issues, but if I was not available, one of the board members or a senior executive would step in.

We also faced challenges in our relationship with the trade unions. For quite a long time, we were ignored by them, but eventually they began to pressure our drivers to join the Transport Union. As management, we had no problem with this, because we were paying our drivers well, and they were all happy with their work environment, so we gave them the choice of joining the union, or not. When 95 percent of our employees voted against the idea, the Storeman and Packers Union boycotted our company, refusing to receive goods from some of the major city stores if they were transported by Veith Transport trucks. Eventually the pressure became too great, and the drivers were forced to join the Transport Union.

Another hassle for us was when interstate carriers were having a slack time in Melbourne. They would quote the local trade very cheaply just to keep their fleet going. As soon as the interstate work became busy again, they dumped the local deliveries. Nevertheless, if we lost clients for this or similar reasons, they almost always returned to us again. It was extremely unusual for us to lose a client in the long term, and this was very encouraging.

Theft is a big temptation in the transport industry, and we often experienced serious problems with theft from dishonest employees.

Sometimes part-time high school or university students who unloaded the trucks at the dock in the afternoon would steal small things, such as cameras and jewellery, as well as larger items, such as television sets. Less often, we would have a dishonest driver who worked in collusion with the dock staff, and we would have to dismiss them.

Theft was also a problem when trucks were left unattended during a delivery. Our trucks used to have a distinctive red Veith sign on a mid-blue background across the side of the vehicle, but this made them easy targets for robbers, who would follow them to Shopping Town in Doncaster, where we had many deliveries of television sets, jewellery and other expensive items. If the driver was careless and left his truck unlocked for a moment, robbers would take everything they could sell cheaply and be gone before the driver returned. It was impossible to trace the goods or get them back.

On one occasion, when a driver was loading up in South Yarra, with his truck backed up to the firm's warehouse door, someone climbed into the driver's seat and drove away with the whole truck, which was fully loaded. When we found it, it was empty. Our margin of profit on most of the parcels we handled was very small, so we needed to carry thousands of them to cover our costs.

Insurance companies rarely covered theft, so we required clients to insure their goods under their own insurance policy on the understanding that we would do our best to see that the goods arrived safely at their destination. But we found this difficult to enforce, because clients would say that this arrangement was not acceptable to them and threaten to take their business elsewhere. So we often had to carry the losses.

During all these years, as we constantly faced challenges and worries, I discovered that I really do have natural business acumen. But the amazing success of the business was due to much more than that. Through all the difficult times, we continued our regular prayer in board and management meetings, and the Lord helped and blessed us in beautiful ways. I also maintained my personal practice of spending time with the Lord each day, and whenever I was unsure about what to do I found surprising and practical answers to my dilemmas. Where I was weak in some area, someone else came along with the right gifts. When circumstances seemed impossible, a way opened that I had not considered. It was a continual and astounding revelation to me, and my heart was full to overflowing every night when we had our family devotions and I looked back on the day and how God had answered so many prayers. This happened so often that I gradually came to expect that God would hear my prayers, and he continued to answer them in marvellous ways.

Whether we pray as a church, a group, or as individuals, this grounded expectation that God will hear our prayers is important. I don't mean that it's not costly, for there is a very real discipline and commitment involved. We really have to mean business with the Lord, that is, to be fair dinkum. I want to encourage others in this, because I have experienced the amazing power and grace of God to answer prayer on a daily basis and to do what seemed impossible.

* * *

While the transport division of Mission Enterprises rapidly expanded during these years, we also began to diversify by initiating creative ministries in Australia and overseas. One of the first was the pastoral division within Mission Enterprises which was inspired by my reading about a program in America called Steer Incorporated, where the company bought baby steers, and farmers volunteered to look after them on their farms, with the company covering any expenses. When the animals were eventually sold, the money went to Steer Incorporated.

A friend of mine had a brother with a large farm near Portland, in western Victoria, and I saw this as a way to support missions, so I visited him with the idea. He was very interested in offering his farm and time to raise cattle, crops, or other animals for Mission Enterprises, which covered all his overhead expenses through its transport business. When the animal or the harvest was sold, Mission Enterprises received the money, and the farmer nominated where to send it. In this way, Christian farmers had the opportunity to raise funds for missions and other projects in Australia and overseas. The project became highly successful, with eventually three hundred farmers participating from every state and territory in Australia, except the Northern Territory, enabling us to give away millions of dollars.

Mission Enterprises employed my brother Wally,[14] who had come back from missionary service in India when his family needed to be back in Australia. He visited each farmer every year to discuss how the project was operating and to learn if they had any suggestions or problems. In doing this he also nurtured a pastoral ministry to the farmers and their families, and as a result he was invited to be a guest preacher in many country churches, an arrangement that blessed everyone. When Wally retired in 1978, Mission Enterprises hired Ken Craig, another returned missionary, who had worked with the Sudan Interior Mission and who had previously been a wheat farmer in New South Wales. Ken had a natural rapport with the farmers, and he also found himself with an informal pastoral ministry in rural Australia. It was a great joy to see how this initiative to engage farmers in the Mission Enterprises dream brought such satisfaction to farmers and to Mission Enterprises.

* * *

In addition to the transport and pastoral divisions of the business, an unexpected encounter led to the development of other creative initiatives. One day, a man I had never met before walked into my office, saying that he felt that the Lord had sent him to me, but he didn't know why. His name was Dirk Bakker (mentioned earlier) and he wanted to know what Mission Enterprises was all about. I began explaining it to him and as we talked, we seemed to establish an easy rapport, and I began to wonder if the Lord had indeed sent him to me, although I was uncertain what it meant.

His background was in business and market management.[15] I respected his wide experience and humility, and his broad view of the Church and its work in the world led me to believe that he would work well within the ethos of Mission Enterprises. I could also see that he had gifts and strengths that I lacked and I felt that we would complement each other in creative ways. The other directors agreed, though none of us had a clear idea about where this new configuration of leadership might lead.

With courage and faith Dirk joined the Mission Enterprises team. He had experience and contacts in many areas which provided new opportunities for us. We looked for situations where there seemed to be a gap, then sought to offer something innovative in that area. Most of these ministries operated for a limited time because of our intentional policy to meet a specific need and then move on to another area when others took up the challenge.

We realised that the leadership teams in most churches, missionary societies, and other Christian organisations had little, if any, formal training in leadership and management. Many small businesses were in a similar position. This was Dirk's area of expertise and so we offered lectures, workshops and seminars in these areas and were inundated with people wanting to participate. We also noticed that as missions, churches or businesses grew, personal conflicts between staff often emerged— particularly at the leadership level. In such situations, Dirk came in as an outsider to help to mediate conflicts from a neutral position. One of his great gifts was the ability to relate to individuals from the grassroots to the top leadership.

Because of this, we soon had invitations from many different missionary groups in Papua New Guinea, where Dirk had personal ties,[16] wanting us to offer management, leadership and cross-cultural training to their leaders and staff in what was a complex situation at a very significant time for missions in the country. Some politicians also availed themselves of this training.

We also realised the difficulties that many missionaries faced in re-adjusting to life in their home country when they returned from overseas service for months of furlough or for longer periods, such as attending to the educational needs of their families, or upon their final return after many years away. Dirk organised meetings to provide them with support for working through culture shock in this disorienting season of transition. He oriented them to the changes in Australian culture and society that had happened while they were away and encouraged them to re-establish relationships, find meaningful employment, and settle into a local church community. At the same time, he affirmed the insights and challenges that they had received from their time in another country and culture and encouraged them to bring this acquired experience to bear on their home culture in enriching ways. When the Evangelical Alliance and other missionary societies began to develop this area of ministry for missionaries returning from the field, we let this go and moved into new areas. We called this wide variety of initiatives the "XYZ division" within Mission Enterprises, and we always sought to be sensitive to the nudges of the Holy Spirit in deciding where we would put our energy and finances.

For instance, we felt called to work in the area of the media and established a group which worked for justice in broadcasting because we were concerned about the media's bias against Christian values and that the control of the media was in too few hands. We worked with politicians, lawyers and concerned others with knowledge in this area, who generously volunteered their time and expertise. Many hours were spent lobbying the Federal Government, heightening awareness of the issues. We also invested time, money and energy to support Christian artists working in many different mediums as we discovered that creative artists are often not adept in management skills. A further program arose out of our concern to encourage and support thoughtful, informed thinking regarding many of the complex issues of contemporary society. We established a resource centre and library, with material on legal and medical ethics at Alphington, a suburb of Melbourne. As we continued to be open to the leading of the Holy Spirit, other initiatives also developed which led to a wave of creative energy which brought life to our work and ourselves as well as others. It was an exciting time.

The wider work of Mission Enterprises continued to support churches, para-church organisations and individuals across Australia. But we also became interested in discovering what the Lord was doing in all parts of the world and how we were called to help bring the Gospel to all people by supporting justice, alleviating poverty and extending the vision of the Kingdom of God. Though the local church is certainly very important, and for this reason I am deeply committed to the ministries and people of my church at Kew, the Lord invited me to embrace a much broader vision, which I shared with my colleagues at Mission Enterprises. At present, we are supporting one hundred and fifty Christian groups in many countries of the world. We try to listen carefully to the invitations of the Holy Spirit, and in following these we have been led into surprising places.

We have certainly come to understand that we cannot preach the Gospel to people who are starving, ill, oppressed, homeless, or suffering trauma, without seeking to help them and without supporting initiatives that will empower them to rebuild their lives and set them free from poverty and debt. We've learned to value the whole Gospel in relation to the well being of the whole person and community, because we believe that these are values of the Kingdom of God. Because of this perspective, we are increasingly supporting Christian organisations such as Tear Fund, Compassion and World Vision, who are sending out professionals trained in business, agriculture, health, education and related vocations, to train, support and empower the poor in developing countries or places ravaged by famine and war. We believe that institutional sin and oppressive, corrupt structures in society must be challenged and that justice must be supported in all places. We want to see real change so that people are released from the cycles of poverty and all its related problems while they are also being nurtured in faith.[17]

At the moment, I am talking with an American group called Frontiers, a relatively new Christian organisation that is committed to following the ways of Jesus and the Kingdom of God amongst the disadvantaged peoples of the world. It is not a missionary society, but is deeply committed to being a witness to the Gospel through the way its people live and work for the welfare of all people in a holistic way, very similar to the vision we have come to embrace at Mission Enterprises. The organisation is drawing together people who feel called to invest time, finances and energy in developing countries in order to generate financial and professional resources that will enable the people and the country to address poverty and structural injustice. For example, they might establish a business in a developing country, but the profits must remain there and be used to develop agriculture, necessary infrastructure, health and education. If we join with Frontiers, it will be an expansion of what we are already doing in many places. Our interests are worldwide, and I suppose there's scarcely a country where Mission Enterprises has not helped in some way. The fact that it is possible for us to do this is a source of deep gratitude to God and a joy to me.

I am also learning about a much smaller organisation in England that has a magazine called "The Third Way," and they have done many things even though they don't have a great deal of money. I find it interesting that here is a group in another country thinking in this way, as if God is touching the hearts of very different people in different lands with a similar call. I find it very exciting and look forward to what may come from it.

It is very moving to recall all the creative energy we felt as these diverse ministries unfolded within Mission Enterprises. I never dreamed that such rich variety would come from such small beginnings. When I was engaged in the hurly-burly of my life—family, church, pastoral visiting and business—with all the pressing decisions to be made, challenges to be met, management and financial concerns, personnel issues and expansion plans, I sometimes lost sight of the miracle it was to watch my "impossible" childhood dream come true in these remarkable and totally unforeseen ways. Sometimes, I can't believe that the business has grown to this place, where we are able to channel all the profits into the Lord's work, but it happened under my nose, a daily wonder. During my reflection times at the close of each day, I am often overwhelmed by the grace and kindness of the Lord, who has helped me in so many ways.

* * *

Reliving the story of the business, which has been such a major part of my life, has been an emotional journey. I sense the wonderful life and creative energy flowing through the surprises of it all. But last night, after settling into my familiar chair in the study for my usual quiet time and prayer, I fell into deep quietness as I began to reflect on God's presence in the day. After a short time, I began to recall my comments about what the business has done in Australia and around the world, and I began to feel increasingly uncomfortable and upset. As it all came back to me in vivid detail, my tears began to flow, and I realised that I may have given a very false picture in my telling of the story. I am so deeply conscious of two essential things that I did not really articulate at all, and I regret that deeply.

The first thing that emerged in my quiet reflection was my awareness of the many times I have missed out on doing good when opportunities have been given to me—perhaps through laziness or a lack of faith. I'm often very conscious of this, and I am distressed that I did not think of mentioning it, for that omission skews the story in some way, which was not my intention.

The second thing that surfaced was the overwhelming sense of God's generous goodness and love, which always enfolds me, in spite of my shortcomings in this area. I cannot begin to express the reality of these experiences adequately, but they are very much a part of my life and are tied up with all that I feel about the astounding way Mission Enterprises has unfolded. In order to tell that story from my perspective, I need to emphasise these things and so bring balance to it. The whole enterprise is really an expression of God's life in me and of my life in God.

***

Timeline of Business

c. 1933–1941 Depression years; beginning of World War II. Eugene inherits old baby Austin 7 and begins delivering for Scott Bros.

c. 1942–1945: World War II continues. Marriage to Ruth in 1942; family home and business both at Wills Street, Kew.

c. 1946–1949: Post-war years. Veith Transport Company established.

c. 1950–1958: Two drivers (Ron Nethercott and Ray Gibbs) with two trucks and a small van, grew to six trucks putting pressure on the available space at Wills Street and on the growing family.

1960–1973: Separation of family home and business, with home at Harp Road, East Kew and Veith Transport, with six trucks at Burwood Road, Hawthorn. Mission Enterprises was established in 1960, sharing the Hawthorn depot site with Veith Transport. The new company had four vehicles bringing the total number now at the depot to ten. The Veith name was also featured on these. By 1973 there were twenty-four trucks and loading bays. During these years, the business operation changed from the early system of a few trucks owned by the business and driven by employee-drivers to sub-contracting work to drivers who owned their own vehicles. Dirk Bakker joined the management team as a director and manager of Mission Enterprises; Stuart Brown joined the management team as a director and marketing and administration manager of the transport division of the company, a role Eugene had undertaken until then in addition to his other responsibilities.

1974–1979: Veith Transport was sold to Mission Enterprises in 1974, becoming a not-for-profit company. Hawthorn depot expanded in 1974 and again in 1979, from the original six trucks and loading bays to thirty-two in 1980. There was also an additional fleet of taxi trucks which did not come to the depot but were operated from there by radio contact; this fleet began with ten and grew to forty-five vehicles. Another fleet of twenty courier vehicles operated in a similar way in the northern suburbs of Melbourne.

1980–1986: After twenty years at Hawthorn the site had become inadequate and the depot was moved to 36 Franklyn Street, Huntingdale, with space for forty-eight trucks and parcel runs. This number soon grew to fifty-six. A new conveyor belt system streamlined the daily unloading, sorting and loading for the next day's deliveries by a simple colour coding system. Before long, there were sixty parcel runs, operating from two depots. The taxi trucks had grown to sixty-five and with the courier fleet there were eventually 180 drivers operating under the Veith name—a familiar sight on Melbourne streets.

1986: As the largest capital city metro parcel organisation in Australia, Mission Enterprises/Veith Transport operated sixty parcel runs and had the capacity to handle 25,000 parcels daily. When they outgrew their operating space yet again, they sold this transport division to Mayne Nicholas, their largest competitor, who agreed to establish a larger depot in Clayton, retain existing staff and directors during the transition and keep the Veith name. The money from the sale went into Mission Enterprises which now became a not-for-profit investment company, committed to giving away its income for the Lord's work in Australia and overseas.

1988–1989: Under Mayne Nicholas, the new Veith Parceline depot opened at 110 Fairbank Road, Clayton—the most modern in Australia and twice the size of the previous depot at Huntingdale. Within a year, they operated 104 trucks and parcel runs.

2008: The Entrust Foundation was established two years before Eugene's death, to widen the ministry of Mission Enterprises and ensure that its mission would continue after his passing. Richard Beaumont, who had joined the Mission Enterprises Board in 2001, was appointed part-time CEO in 2008, a position that became full-time in 2011, which he still holds in 2016.

Endnotes

1 Rolheiser, Ronald. *Against an Infinite Horizon: The Finger of God in Our Everyday Lives.* New York: Crossroad, revised edition, 2001, 9.

2 Prior to this Eugene was sole proprietor of a family business.

3 Ron Nethercott and Ray Gibbs were the two drivers, and both remained with the company until they retired. Ron became a significant member of the management team, one of the directors of Mission Enterprises Board and company secretary. Ron sometimes thought Eugene was too soft with his employees, and at times he stepped in to rectify this. But Ron also was remarkably concerned for the welfare of all the drivers and their families, often spending time listening to their concerns and seeking ways of helping them.

4 Adjoining land and buildings were purchased or rented several times during this period. The number of trucks and loading bays grew from six in 1959, to ten in 1960, to twenty-four in 1973, and to thirty-two in 1980. The office space was also enlarged several times in this period.

5 ASIC Registration was in August 1960. The new company had a board of directors, and the documents were signed by Eugene Veith, Ruth Veith, Barrie Paul and Ron Nethercott.

6 For example, a shop-fitting business and a large-scale mobile curtain cleaning business.

7 During these years Stuart Brown and Dirk Bakker joined Ron Nethercott and Eugene as directors. Ron and Stuart were involved in the management, marketing and day to day running of the transport division of the business, while Dirk was involved in the management, implementation and leadership of the wider program of Mission Enterprises, loosely described as the XYZ division. Their commitment, expertise and hard work complemented Eugene's vision in remarkable ways. Ron remained a significant part of the business for many years; Stuart Brown became an integral part of the management team until the business was sold to Mayne Nicholas. He continued to hold positions on the board for many years, and he is currently (2016) chair of the board of Mission Enterprises. Dirk has also continued his involvement in a variety of ways, including being a director.

8 Veith Transport was sold to Mission Enterprises for $150,000 in 1974.

9 From the early 1960's the business operated by sub-contracting work to drivers who owned their own trucks. A driver would come to the depot, pack his truck, depart to deliver his load to different locations, and then pick up new cargo from warehouses and other places to be unloaded for sorting in the evening at the depot dock. This was called the daily parcel run.

10 In our conversations, Eugene became very animated as he told me about the move to Huntingdale and how the new plant streamlined the efficiency of the business operations. In the afternoons, as the trucks returned to the depot, the drivers pre-sorted their parcels as they unloaded them onto a unique colour-coded, floor-level steel conveyor belt. Dock staff removed the parcels from the other side of the conveyor belt and placed them in the colour-coded holding bays. With this simple system, each driver had a specific area for his parcel run and a colour-coded bay that held the goods and paperwork necessary for his parcel run the following day.

11 One of the company's major competitors.

12 Eugene retired after three months; Ron Nethercott remained until August 1988; Stuart Brown remained until March 1989.

13 Today, these activities are better known as the Entrust Foundation, which is owned by Mission Enterprises Victoria. See www.entrust.org.au and associated links.

14 Walter and his wife had previously spent many years in India as missionaries, and Eugene was very sensitive to the struggles they faced as a family and in establishing their ministry. This gave a strong personal impetus to Eugene's dream of supporting missionaries and their ministries.

15 Dirk was the Australian representative of the Dale Carnegie Institute and had wide experience in business and market management. At this time, he was feeling drawn towards more specifically Christian work. While praying about this, he felt prompted to go and visit Eugene and learn more about Mission Enterprises.

16 These included the Christian Leaders Training College, Australian Baptist Missionary Society, the Nazarenes, Lutherans, Seventh Day Adventists and others.

17 For Eugene there was no division between his passion for justice and his deep communion with and love for God. This is characteristic of the mystical tradition when it is most authentic. For example, the Quaker Thomas Kelly (1893–1941), who had his own personal experience of being literally "melted down by the love of God," writes: "The straightest road to social gospel runs through profound mystical experience. The paradox of true mysticism is that individual experience leads to social passion…If we seek a social gospel we must find it in the mystic way. Love of God and love of neighbor are not two commandments, but one." From Thomas Kelly, *The Eternal Promise*, cited in *Quaker Spirituality: Selected Writings*, edited by Douglas Steer. Mahwah, NJ: Paulist Press, 1984, 306.

VI

Every moment and every event of every man's life on earth plants something in his soul. For just as the wind carries thousands of invisible and visible winged seeds, so the stream of time brings with it germs of spiritual vitality that come to rest imperceptibly in the minds and wills of men. Most of these unnumbered seeds perish and are lost, because men are not prepared to receive them: for such seeds as these cannot spring up anywhere except in the good soil of liberty and desire.

–Thomas Merton, *Seeds of Contemplation*[1]

Tending the seeds of healing

For I will restore health to you, and your wounds I will heal, says the Lord.
-Jeremiah 30:17 NRSV

The seeds of intercessory prayer for healing, both for myself and others, were sown in my earliest years on the Yarragon farm, when I imbibed my father's faith in divine healing. In the years that followed, my interest in healing developed very naturally and quietly, refined and modified by my growing and maturing faith. This interest has never been merely academic, but rather the experience of being called toward healing in one way or another most of my life. During my teens and early adulthood, my experiences of disability and poor health, as well as the reprehensible 'faith healing' practices I observed amongst some people, fostered within me a deep compassion for those suffering from ill-health, while also shaping my understanding of the mystery of healing.

During those formative years, I became very fond of bike riding and competed at various levels. In the mornings, I trained for this by running around the local oval, and I became quite good at the sport. By my early twenties, I began to notice that I could ride well on the flat, but when I had to pedal uphill I began puffing and panting. This difficulty began to afflict me during any strenuous work. I was advised to seek medical help and went to a top Melbourne specialist—a Collins Street man. After taking an x-ray of my heart, he informed me that I had two leaking valves and my heart was enlarged by twenty-five percent. He gave me a bit of a fright, ordering me not to do any heavy work, nor to rush around, nor walk upstairs and said I must lie down after every meal. This was a pretty daunting regime for a young bloke. He also referred me to a local doctor in Kew for six-monthly check-ups and said that if I took it easy, I should be all right. He didn't say for how long, and he didn't give me any medicine. Though it was difficult, I endeavoured to follow his orders. And I prayed about my ticker, but nothing changed.

Meanwhile, I married Ruth and continued to develop my transport business. Because we were starting a family and I was not insured, I went to two or three different companies to secure a good insurance policy, but they all knocked me back on account of my heart. During this time, the

Second World War broke out, and I was called up to enlist in the army, but they refused to take me for the same reason—my heart. Later, after the Japanese entered the war and began invading Papua New Guinea, the army recalled the men they had previously rejected. They re-examined seventy of us from the Kew area—some fellows had one leg, some were crippled, and all the others had some kind of disability. Beside them, I had no obvious physical problems, yet I was one of eight or nine men who were rejected— on account of my heart condition.

Eugene's Medical Certificate of Unfitness to go to war - courtesy of the Veith family

I continued to go to the doctor for regular check-ups and tried to keep to the regime of rest and little exercise, assuming this would be necessary for the rest of my life. Then one day, when I reported for my half-year review, he examined me and said, "Mr Veith, I don't understand this, but I can't find anything wrong with your heart now. Whatever was wrong is gone. Your heart appears to have cured itself. I don't know how." He remained puzzled. One six-monthly check I had the problem, and by the next one, it was gone—and I haven't had it since.

After that, I went back to the insurance company and had no trouble obtaining insurance. Since then, many different doctors—younger than I—have told me during medical examinations that they wished they had my heart. My heartbeat dropped to sixty beats a minute and in the mornings, before I got up, it would be forty-eight, which is apparently that of a top athlete. I can't help laughing about it—the whole thing is very funny. Only five or six years ago, my local doctor concluded his examination by saying, "Keep up the training!" I exclaimed, "I don't do any training!" He found that very hard to believe.

So my fervent, faithful prayers to avert youthful baldness remained unanswered, and my few prayers concerning my heart were answered after many years of simply accepting it as a lifelong problem and living around it. To be honest, I hadn't really prayed about it for a long time and had given up asking. Perhaps I reached this point of acceptance much sooner with my heart, because I already had years of unanswered prayer about my hair and stammer. Regardless, my unexpected experience of healing left me with an overwhelming sense of gratitude and a continuing desire to be involved in this mysterious ministry in quiet, gentle, prayerful ways, open to learning and open to God.

Although this experience increased my faith in divine healing, I was left with as many questions as answers. Obviously there was no simple formula, for I had also experienced the anguish of unanswered prayers for healing through long periods of deep disappointment and suffering. Other people used to say, "Surely God could have sent you just one of these afflictions instead of all three?" or, "It's not fair," or, "Why do you think he's done that?" On and on the questions would go.

In spite of this, I remember well the spontaneous pleasure I had in noticing that I did not blame the Lord for my misfortunes. Even then, those comments did not resonate with my growing experience of God.

* * *

The seeds of healing prayer took deeper root in my life as I prayed in this way for myself and my family in the ordinary routines of our lives. Over time, when a friend or someone in the church would ask for healing prayer, I would pray for them as well. Then in 1968, the Reverend Peter Manton came to Kew Baptist, and he invited me and a few others to join him in praying for individuals, families, or small groups in our congregation whenever they asked for healing prayer. Our little group gathered once a week to read, reflect and pray about this ministry, and our time together quickened my interest in healing prayer and gave me the wisdom and confidence to continue this naturally in other spheres of my life.

Through the years, I developed an informal visitation routine with people I met through my business and other activities, and this became part of the rhythm of my life. I would pray with the people I visited as a natural part of our conversation, and if they asked for specific healing prayer, then I would pray for them in that way.

As I consider these roots of healing prayer in my life, I'm recalling some particular encounters with people who were ill and suffering and how their deep need and the prayers given to them became a doorway into a life of faith. One man had such a bad back that he was unable to work, and he asked me to pray for him. He was not a person of faith at the time, but he was willing to try anything to find healing for his back. Healing came to him, and through that experience, he came to faith in Christ.

When people are sick or in pain, their suffering often opens them to God, even if they are not overtly people of faith and prayer. Sometimes an unbeliever is healed and a person of deep faith is not. There are many questions in this ministry, and no one knows all the answers. But even when physical healing does not occur, there is frequently a deep inner healing of mind and spirit and also of relationships. And sometimes quickly, sometimes slowly, there may also be incredible physical healing in a person's life.

I remember a woman of faith who was not a member of Kew Baptist asking our small prayer group to come and pray with her. She had a blood condition that was causing her trouble, and her sight was deteriorating. We went and prayed with her three times. The last time, only two of us could go because she called us urgently on a Friday afternoon. We were with her about twenty minutes.

The following Monday, I phoned to ask how she was and to encourage her through this difficult time, as was my usual practice after we prayed with someone. She told me that an hour or so before we arrived on Friday, she knew that she was going to be healed. Then she had a big battle with

God about her internal feelings of hatefulness towards someone, and she realised that she had to deal with this before she could be healed. During this hard wrestling, she remembered the story of Jacob wrestling with God all night by the river Jabbok.[2] Finally, she had a sense of victory.

After we prayed with her, she went into her bedroom and saw things that she had not seen for ages, because her sight had been so poor. A few days later, she had an appointment with a specialist concerning her blood condition, and he found her blood was normal. I spoke to her several years after this incident, and she is still in excellent health and active in the life of her church community.

This experience moved me and gave me an insight into the interconnection between our bodies, minds and spirits, particularly how grudges, resentment, hate and unforgiveness can erode our health. Through the experience of healing prayer, this lady became aware of what was hindering her healing and harming her health, though she did not speak about this to us in the earlier meetings we had with her or on that Friday afternoon. When God touched her with this clear awareness, she found the inner courage to confront her hatred.

We are invited not only to encourage each other in faith, but also to admonish each other gently in love.[3] So if I have a problem in my life to which I am blind, and you can see it, then I think that you are under the obligation of the Lord's love in you to tell me: "Eugene, I think you are a little bit out of line here." We are told to tell each other the truth in love and to be thankful when someone cares enough for us to tell us that we are wrong about something,[4] for then we can learn and change for the better. In this way, the ministry of wise admonition is sometimes related to the ministry of healing because my blind behaviour or attitudes may be part of my sickness. But we are scared to do this for each other, because it can sound judgemental. And though we need to be cautious, this is a ministry that we neglect to our detriment—provided we remember that we are not to judge one another. For it is true we might do great harm to people if we are wrong in our discernment or if we admonish them for the wrong reasons. As in all things balance is important, and in this instance we must hold the importance of encouragement in tandem with the gentle ministry of correction.

When I am invited to pray for someone's healing, I am always conscious of how much I don't know about it all. We cannot simply assume that when healing does not occur, there is some inner wounding of the spirit that needs healing before physical healing will follow. Some of the greatest saints have not been healed. Sometimes, a person is healed of one thing and not another—as in my case, when my heart was healed, but my hair falling out was not. We can only entrust the person we are praying for to God's goodness and allow Him to work. Sometimes what I pray for is not the primary issue—though I don't realise that, and the person concerned may not either—so I always pray that the Lord will bring deliverance into every aspect of a person's life.

* * *

Though there is much we don't understand about healing, and we don't always engage this ministry wisely or well, praying for the sick is one way of doing God's will in the world today. Scripture exhorts us to pray for the sick;[5] it was a hallmark of Jesus' life and faith, and the church should always include prayers for the sick and suffering as a normal part of its worship. But some people are called to healing prayer as a particular ministry, and I am very grateful for and humbled by how this ministry has been such a natural part of my life for many years now.

Recently, I had a sore neck and shoulder, which continued to get worse over a week or more. On Sunday night when I went to bed, it was throbbing painfully, particularly in one spot. I couldn't go to sleep—and normally nothing stops me going to sleep. So I asked the Lord, "would you please take away this pain and touch me?" Almost immediately—I'd say within twenty seconds or so—this throbbing in my shoulder stopped, then started, then hesitated and finally stopped, and I went to sleep. I was interested in the way it stopped and started and then sort of staggered on and off a bit and then finally stopped. I slept peacefully through the night, and in the morning I had no soreness in my shoulder at all. I was free of pain the next week, but in the last few days I had a touch of it —and now it's gone after I asked the Lord about it. This is an illustration of how healing prayer is a natural part of my wider life of faith and prayer, from the small things to the big things.

* * *

As I reflect on my journey, I find myself drawn to ask how I have come to know God more deeply through the practice of healing prayer and how this has shaped me both inwardly and outwardly. But it is very humbling to try and convey what I am feeling, because my words seem inadequate, fuzzy, blurred. I cannot bridge this gap between my experience of God and my words, so the effort seems futile. But as I allow this awareness to unfold gently within me, I can see that I need to hold these contradictory truths in tension—allowing the experience to deepen within me, whilst also accepting that I can never fully articulate the richness of it.

Remembering now the suffering I experienced during those long periods of disappointment over my unanswered prayers for the healing of my youthful baldness, I am feeling again the anguish that enveloped me back then. When you're a young boy of fifteen, and you're faced with the diagnosis that your weirdly advancing bald patches will progress until you're bald as a bat, it's a terrible shock, and I can still feel that wound keenly. My young adult years were heavy with the dread of this finality, and yet always tinged with the hope that it wouldn't happen, that I would be healed. My tears come easily, and I am surprised by the intensity and depth of the feeling for the young person I still carry inside me. It makes me wonder if that old wound still needs to be healed, or if it is operating in me in unhealthy ways.

But as I reflect prayerfully on this experience, I do not believe that this wound is still open and bleeding, refusing to heal. Rather, I think I have found some pretty healthy scar tissue there! The strong, tearful emotion is a powerful surge of compassion for my youthful self as I come alongside and embrace him now as an old man. Amidst the recognition of this compassionate stream washing over my younger self, a slim shaft of light has surfaced in my consciousness. This unexpected awareness of a river-like stream of compassion flowing backwards and forwards through my life seems like a mixture of God and my older self, flowing together in lovingkindness that is gentle and healing.

To my surprise, I realise that what I have so unexpectedly seen in my own life is the same experience I have when I talk or pray with people who are suffering, or seeking some sort of healing. It is not just a feeling of sympathy or pity, but a deep sense of compassionate solidarity *with* them, a concern for their wellbeing in every way. This compassionate 'withness' has a strength that surprises me, and it helps me to hold the person into the mystery of God's presence which enfolds us both so that I never feel as if I am drowning in their suffering.

In this situation I experience God's love intensely, and this not only draws me closer to the people I am praying with, but also to the Lord. I feel the same sense of 'withness'—or empathy—with him, and in this I have experienced another dimension of the love of God. It is as if I am being given a little peep into something more of God's very being—a window of insight into the gospel, myself, all people, all that is. This divine-human stream of compassion and tender love is flowing back and forth through my own life with healing energy,[6] and it courses through me to others and back again. It's not that I don't experience this sense of God's presence at other times—driving the car, or anywhere, really—but during healing prayer, it is more focused and intense.

As always, my words cannot convey the vividness of these times of intercessory prayer. I don't know how to talk about what is there—with me, behind me, before me—as I try to evoke with these futile little descriptions, the beauty of God being in empathy with us, being *for* us in our suffering and struggles, our vulnerability, our lack of understanding, our humanness. All suffering is held in God, and the cross is a doorway through which we are drawn into the life of God. I am overwhelmed with wonderment that the great Creator bends so low, becoming one with us and permeating the whole creation in tender healing ways.

Most of the time we live only half-awake to the reality that God—the Mystery behind all and in all—is with us, drawing near to us through the ordinariness of everyday life. What a strange paradox! But in times of suffering, or when we share the suffering of others in healing prayer, we may sense God's closeness in a clearer way as our awareness and sensibilities are heightened. In our extremity and helplessness, we frequently awaken to his surprising mercy.

I feel blessed by my experience of divine compassion through healing prayer, because it has brought me closer to the Lord, and it has given me a growing understanding and compassion towards people who are not well. It has also made me sharply aware of how much I do not know and how deeply I need the wisdom that comes from above. I live with many unanswered questions, but also with immense gratitude to God for drawing me so closely to himself and to others in this way.

I hope to remain active in the ministry of healing prayer as I continue to age, because it takes me into the heart of God and into the hearts of people in a very down- to- earth sort of way. I continue to have a deep reverence and confidence in the active, healing presence of God amongst us.

Endnotes

1 Thomas Merton: *Seeds of Contemplation*. New York: Dell, 1957, 11.

2 Genesis 32:22–32.

3 Colossians 3:16.

4 Ephesians 4:15.

5 James 5:14–16.

6 Eugene frequently spoke in this way about his intercessions for people generally, although he felt it in a heightened way in healing prayer. The Orthodox Archbishop Anthony Bloom describes a similar experience in the prayer of Father Silouan for the young workers in his charge when he was at Mount Athos: "In the beginning I prayed with tears of compassion for Nicholas, for his young wife, for the little child, but as I was praying the sense of the divine presence began to grow on me...it grew so powerful that I lost sight of Nicholas, his wife, his child, his needs, their village, and I could be aware only of God, and I was drawn deeper and deeper, until of a sudden, at the heart of this presence I met the divine love holding Nicholas, his wife and his child, and now it was with the love of God that I began to pray for them again, but again I was drawn into the deep and in the depths of this I again found the divine love. Noted in John V. Taylor, *The Go-Between God*. Minneapolis, MN: Fortress, 1973, 233.

VII

The most important thing for you is your vision, your sense of God whom your work must glorify. The richer, deeper, wider, truer your vision of Divine Reality the more real, rich and fruitful your work is going to be. You must feel the mysterious attraction of God, His loveliness and wonder, if you are ever going—in however simple a way—to impart it to others.

–Evelyn Underhill, *A Companion on Many Journeys*[1]

The mysterious attraction of God

Simon son of John, do you love me?" He said to him, "Yes, Lord; you know
that I love you." Jesus said to him, "Tend my sheep."

John 21:16 NRSV

In my early years of faith, I was very lacking in confidence and though
I was passionate about evangelism I expressed this largely by putting my
energy into the organisational aspect of things because I was very good at
that. But as I've matured more in the Christian life and its inner depths,
the Lord has given me a greater understanding of human nature and a
greater confidence which has drawn me into personal ministry with a wide
diversity of people who are journeying with God in different ways. My
longing is for each person to know how much they are loved by God and to
be supported as they grow in their own love of God.

Whenever I visit those whom God has drawn into my life, I try to listen,
without hurrying them along, encouraging them wherever they are. I try
to leave space for the Lord to work in each of us. Then I pray with them, if
they ask for that, and later, during my private reflection, I continue to hold
them in prayer. As I do this, the Spirit of God gives me insight and helps
me to appreciate where each person is and how I may help him or her, and
then I wait to see how the Lord will sustain and guide each one. I keep in
touch regularly, but what is most important to me is that everyone I meet
will sense God's love coming to them through me. And that is entirely the
work of the Spirit. In many ways, I receive as much as I give from all of these
different people. They teach me a great deal, and I meet God in them.

Though this gift has developed over the years of my life, I can recall early
signs of it when I was a young teenager, helping my father in his butcher's
shop in Malvern. The Lord gave me a love of people back then, and as I rode
my bicycle around the streets to deliver meat to our different customers, I
really enjoyed my interactions with them. Even though I was very confused
and painfully shy, I was able to sense where they were and the best way to
interact with them.

I have been remembering one particular moment of this awareness
from my early years. When I was living through that agonizing time in

Kensington, we lived next door to a girl named Eva, and I really liked her. To myself, I called her my girlfriend, though I am not aware that she ever reciprocated that feeling. In spite of how much I liked her, I was thrilled when we moved away from the school and peer group where I'd been so miserable. A few years later, when I was seventeen, I made my foundational decision to really trust God. I was working in the butcher's shop in Malvern and really wanting to mean business with the Lord. Though we had left Kensington quite some time before, I repeatedly felt moved to go back and tell Eva about the Lord, for she had no religious background and had a very difficult father. Even though I was painfully shy and lacking in confidence, I finally phoned her and made a date with her.

By this time I had my driver's licence, and one Sunday morning I drove all the way to Kensington and brought her back to our place for lunch. When I took her home, I told her about the Lord in a stumbling sort of way, utterly convinced that I was failing and spoiling everything. But when I phoned her later on, she astonished me by saying that my words had made a big impact on her.

Over the years many similar experiences have given me greater confidence in God, and I don't agonise so much about my painful feelings of inadequacy. My mother had a similar gift in relating to many different kinds of people, and I think I inherited this ability from her. So the seeds of my present love for people were in me from an early age, and as my faith matured and my experience of God's love deepened, my love for people grew. Since then, I have learned more and become more confident in God. I enjoy watching what God does in people's lives, but it is still a great surprise when they say how much it means to them that I visit, because it all seems so simple and natural.[2]

From early on, the Lord gave me a love for Scripture as well as for people, and as I became more confident in God, my meditations on his Word continued to build me up in faith and at the same time to teach me about how to relate to others in meaningful ways. As a young person, I was able to grasp spiritual insights at a fairly deep level, even though I had little assurance and was not gifted to expound the Scriptures through preaching. But in most areas of my life, I have been able to see what is essential, and I can get to the core of things without getting distracted or sidetracked. This ability which helped me in business has also helped me in my relationships with people.

My most significant early encouragement in personal ministry came through my sister Olive and her work at Benwerrin, where hundreds of women have been helped and many have found faith. After the birth of Olive's second child, she became very ill and never forgot how terribly difficult it all was. She decided that one day she would like to have a place where women could have time out to receive rest and be nourished with warmth and good food and, if they wished, receive spiritual guidance.

Benwerrin - courtesy of the Veith family

In 1951, she and her husband accepted an invitation to manage Benwerrin, a Christian guesthouse which consisted of a lovely rambling old house on two acres of land, nestled amongst the beautiful hills of Yarra Junction alongside the Little Yarra River. From that time onwards, Olive and her husband were connected with the place in a number of different ways and ministries. Eventually, the "time out" guest house became a place of refuge for traumatised women and children who were escaping from family violence and were often referred there by police and hospitals.

I have always taken a great personal interest in my sister's dream for Benwerrin, and it is an ongoing joy for me that with the support of Mission

Enterprises, she has been able to make her vision a reality. Because Olive could not possibly follow up with everyone who came to Benwerrin, she asked if I would help her.[3] Generally, I'm not in favour of men doing one-to-one ministry with women, because for obvious reasons I think it's better for women to do it. However, because Olive asked for my support, I began following up with those she suggested—and often with their husbands too—praying with them and helping to establish them in their faith or offering practical assistance as needed. This has been an ongoing commitment for me, and I have enjoyed it and learned a great deal through it.

***

Gradually, my visitation extended beyond Benwerrin to include other people I met in the course of my life, particularly through my business and church, and I was able to help both believers and non-believers in practical ways or by listening to them when they were in hard places. Through all of this, I have grown to realise that the best and most natural expression of my concern for people comes through my one-to-one encounters. Part of me would have liked to be a preacher, but because I was so lacking in confidence, that has not been my gift. Over the years, I have gained more experience, and this has strengthened my confidence in the presence of God's outflowing love through me to whoever I am with and whatever their need. Perhaps because I feel so much for the person I am with, the love of God comes out, even through my faltering speech.

I remember years ago, a man said to me, "You know Eugene, that was the day of my conversion, the day when you spoke to me." I was so surprised, because I had felt so unsure about what to say. People seem to see that I really love them in the Lord, and I think that they sense God's love for them coming through me. So often, I am surprised by the way that some very little thing I have done proves to be very powerful for someone else, a turning point in life. It is the Lord who is with us enabling all this and I am often overwhelmed by the kindness of his presence.

When I began to meet with people who were starting out in their faith, both through Kew Baptist Church as well as other Christian organisations, I simply came alongside them to listen and to help them in their fledgling faith however they wished. I encouraged them to get involved in their community of faith, or I helped them find one and prayed that they would get the support they needed. As my one-to-one ministry with people grew,

I found that people genuinely appreciated me connecting with them in this way. While I would try to engage with a person where they were and not where I thought they should be, it often emerged that they would like some teaching about life and faith, prayer and the Word. So I tried to listen to each person and to the Spirit in us and to follow that as best I could.

When we walk alongside others, we need to hear where they are and begin there. Although God has so much more for us than we could ever expect or imagine, we need to move forward slowly, one step at a time. Sometimes people tell me they don't have enough faith to pray for the big things that are troubling them, so I encourage them to start where they are: "if you haven't got the faith to pray for that big thing, pray for something that's small." This has often proved really helpful, and I've been pleased when some have told me years later, "Eugene, I put that advice you gave me into action and it worked!"

I believe that with new Christians, I must be particularly careful to encourage them, for it can be destructive for mature Christians to speak too much about their faith and experience to those who are not long on the journey. It is easy to forget how the Lord has been working with us for many years and what we have become through the sweat, blood and tears of life—as well as the joy. I am so aware of how all of the bumbling along in my life has been permeated by the mercy and grace of God. To speak of where I am now in faith may make a person young in faith feel hopeless, as though this life is impossible, because they may feel so far from the experiences I describe. So I'm very aware that it is important to be sensitive to another's experience and to be open to listening to God before I speak too much.[4]

If a new Christian is told to spend an hour a day in prayer, it may seem daunting and impossible. The person might try to pray, and when it doesn't work, he may feel discouraged and guilty, thinking, "I'm no good, I don't seem to be what I should be, I can't do this." Then the ground is fertile for the devil to make him feel hopeless. So I say, "Listen, don't worry about the hour—try five minutes. After that, you can add a couple of minutes each day." Then I keep a sympathetic eye on him, and I visit him and listen to his questions, and I pray for him.

I have learned how important it is to understand that new converts who come from outside the church and don't have a family or faith community to support them often have a difficult time finding a church where they feel at home and at ease. The typical middle-class church can be very alienating for single parents, or for those who are divorced, struggling with unemployment, have financial difficulties, a drinking problem or other addiction, or wear clothes that are in need of mending. Because the language, dress, music and interests of the people in most churches might be unfamiliar to them, they feel out of place and struggle to connect in a meaningful way, even if the congregation tries to be welcoming and hospitable. Because of this dilemma, I have found that personal ministries are important ways to nurture those who want and need teaching on faith, prayer and reading the scriptures until they can find a place where they feel confident enough to join in. Sometimes this is a long process.

In my ministry with people, I try to come alongside them and to encourage them to listen to the voice of God's Spirit. For the voice of God's Spirit within us is gentle and encouraging, rather than condemning and debilitating. Mind you, if we want to make progress in faith, we also have to recognize the importance of repentance from sin in our everyday living—and the Holy Spirit can be very firm in challenging or convicting us for stepping out of line or for nursing destructive attitudes, thoughts or behaviours. But the call is always to life and hope, not to despair and a downward spiral of hopelessness.

So when I step out of line with the Lord, I hope the Spirit will really nudge me—strongly if necessary—to notice what I am doing, and I also hope that fellow believers who care for me will draw me aside and reflect their concern. Occasionally, we may need to express our love for one other by correcting or challenging each other in loving, truthful and appropriate ways. We need both carefulness and wisdom—and courage.

Every so often, this gentle correction is a component of the conversation and prayer I share with those I visit. As I listen to the Spirit within them, I sometimes offer my reflection on something that they may not be noticing. For example, sometimes people say, "Eugene, I'd love to know God and to follow him, and yet I like having my own way." When this happens, it is very important for me to make it absolutely clear that you have to make a deliberate choice of the will. For people can have the desire for God, but not be willing to give up their own destructive attitudes or actions. One lady said, "Eugene I'm not prepared to do what the Lord requires of me. I'll stick to my old life." Though she had already decided to follow Christ, it became clear to both of us during our visits that she did not want this life of surrender to God's will, and I respect that. It's her decision.

For these reasons, it is important to walk alongside people after they make a decision to follow Jesus, because conversions can be superficial. Even though I spend most of my time encouraging people, sometimes it becomes clear that I have to be honest about sin and repentance. For example, when people are clearly not living in line with God's ways, I have to call them to turn away from some things and towards God, who is not waiting to hit them with a hammer, but rather inviting them to a better way. This call to ongoing moments of repentance is central to our faith and to our deepening life in God. With others, their conversion is real, but their maturity in faith takes a long time. So it is very important to be patient, gentle and encouraging, because the Lord needs time to deal with us all.

There are others already along the road of faith who are well informed about Scripture, very familiar with biblical passages and the content of the major doctrines of the faith, as well as the arguments for and against the existence of God. Though this knowledge can be important, it can also be a hindrance to a deeper knowledge of God, a knowledge of the heart and spirit as well as the mind, whereas some who are unlearned in many things have a deep heart knowledge of God. I remember a college professor telling me once that a simple girl we both knew had more faith and a more profound understanding of God than he had. The true hallmarks of godliness are humility, meekness (gentle strength) and love, which are the fruits of knowing God and were very clear in Jesus.[5]

There are also those who are restless or seeking to deepen their faith, and they often feel lonely, confused and disheartened. I remember the pain of these times in my own life and my lifelong gratitude for those who quietly came alongside and supported me by listening to me. These are crisis times, because some will give up the struggle, but those who press on will grow into deeper faith. Because of this, I have always tried to listen carefully to the Spirit's leading when I meet with people and to support them in their struggle.

When I visit and pray with mature Christians whose paths have crossed mine over the years, I listen to how they are and encourage them. Many are leaders in ministry who carry heavy loads of responsibility and have few people with whom they can share their lives at a deep level. The role of leader is often lonely, and I have found that many appreciate my coming alongside with a listening heart and the offer to pray with them. For many years, I met regularly in an informal way with whoever was the incumbent minister of Kew Baptist Church and prayed with him informally, offering support and encouragement in this way.

I continued these times of prayer fellowship during the ministry of the Reverend Peter Manton and they were deeply significant for both of us. During Peter's ministry, I was also invited to become a member of the small pastoral group[6] that met weekly to pray for people and to discuss visitation and pastoral care of the church community. Through this group, I engaged in regular pastoral visitation of members of the congregation, which I had been doing informally for many years, but now was sharing with others in an intentional way. I learned a great deal from our regular times of prayer, discussion and teaching, and I appreciated being part of a small team dedicated to caring for people. This was a very important aspect of my life, and it influenced my development in significant ways.

While Peter was the minster at Kew, more than ten men[7] entered theological college and went on to ordination and a subsequent pastoral vocation. In the last few years of Peter's ministry, we would go away for a week or so to visit each of these men and their families, wherever they were serving around the state as well as in the city. We wanted to hear how they were, pray with them and discover if there was any practical help we or the church could offer. Between ourselves, we referred to these times as "Bishop's Tours." Since Baptists do not have bishops as part of their ecclesial structure, it was a way of holding what we were attempting lightly, yet also reverencing the centuries old tradition of offering pastoral care for pastors.

During these times, while Peter and I were out on the road taking a break from the regular routines of our busy lives, we talked as we drove, and we laughed and prayed, feeling really happy to have this opportunity of fellowship and encouragement with these young families. It was a relaxed time, when those we visited could talk about both the struggles and blessings of their vocation, a time when we shared laughter and tears. As we listened and prayed with them, they were encouraged and refreshed within themselves, often receiving healing of some sort through the love and support they received from us as representatives of their home church community. When Peter died so suddenly and unexpectedly, I missed this rich fellowship, along with so many other things, very much.[8]

***

But I don't have adequate words to describe how my experience of God has formed my love of people. With my letter writing, people tell me they're like skeletons without any flesh—just the basics and that's about all. This is another way of saying that I get to the heart of things without many distractions along the way. Because I struggle so much to express my inner thoughts and the deep stirrings of my heart, it strikes me as rather humorous and amazing that I am attempting to reflect like this in my old age.

During my times of communion with God, I feel great joy and wonderment, but mixed in with that is what I can only say is an overwhelming feeling of appreciation for God himself. Appreciation is such an inadequate word, but I mean an all encompassing valuing of God that is not just a feeling, but more like a very moving vision of God's beauty and loveliness, a revelation of God's nature. These words sound drab and lifeless, and I can't seem to bridge the gap between the vivid experience and my flat description.

What I am struggling to articulate is that my overwhelming experience of the infinite love of God seems to flow into my becoming aware of God in everything around me—the people, trees, sky, animals. I go into the desert in the heart of our country—sand, rocks, mountains in the distance, desert everywhere—and I see God's handiwork and beauty in it all. I contemplate the wonder of an animal—a horse, for instance, or the way God has made the human body, which is marvellous. If I stop to look and reflect, everything becomes a way of my seeing God, and an overwhelming love for everyone and everything sweeps over me.[9]

Usually I am on a fairly even keel emotionally, but when this occurs, if I happen to be in a public place, the feeling is so strong that I have to restrain myself from going down the street and putting my arms around people. I have to be careful and watch where I am going when I cross the street so as not to get run over![10] Sometimes, the Lord gives me such a burden for people that I weep for them, though they would never know this or the longing I have to embrace them. But I understand the compassion and tender love that sometimes filled Jesus when he was with people or looking at a crowd.

The essential core of our faith is that we are to love God with all our heart and soul and mind and strength and love our neighbour as ourselves. This is the basic will of God for us all, and it has many applications for everyday living. Throughout each day, I ask myself, "How should I behave under these circumstances?" This question is always before me, and I turn it over in my mind while meditating on the Scriptures in order to be open to God's Word and Spirit.

Now that I am older, God is seldom out of my awareness, and so I am habitually aware of other people for whom I have some kind of concern or relationship. My awareness of God brings me to this deeper awareness of others, and I forget myself completely. I don't think to myself, "I must love people and be self-forgetful," but as I contemplate the Lord, I can't help remembering them also. In the New Testament epistles, the apostle Paul talks often of the love he has for those to whom he is writing and his longing for their welfare. I can understand this, because I really love to see people flourishing in body, mind and spirit. The more I give in love to other people, the more God becomes very real to me. The two go together.

I've noticed that if I'm out of step with the Lord, I lose this sort of thing. It's not something I have all the time, but the degree to which I keep my mind on the Lord affects the depth of my love for other people, and this flows on to my loving God more. But when I see situations in which I feel utterly helpless, when there is really nothing I can do, I sometimes experience emotional distress and turmoil, and I realise that I have to leave these situations in the Lord's hands and wait to see how God will work without worrying over it all too much. I have to come to that place of relinquishment.

The whole of life becomes interesting and fulfilling when I become aware of the surprising ways that the Lord works in baffling circumstances. And sometimes there are problems that never seem to be resolved, and I have to learn to find the Lord's presence there as well. The more I go on with the Lord, the more conflict I have with the powers of darkness, and I have come to realize that I am in a battle and prayer is a sword. The description of the whole armour of God in Ephesians[11] describes this experience very vividly, and I have come to appreciate its practical advice about how to face these battles.

Sometimes the Lord must deal with me in a firm way, and this can be uncomfortable. I may be rather afraid of what is being asked of me, and I may want to avoid it. I've noticed that if I am out of step with the Lord, I lose the depth of my love for others, and this inhibits the flow of my love toward God and my awareness of God's love for me. For it is really one movement—the flow of God's love shed abroad in our hearts[12] and the realisation that everything is from God, which evokes in me a very natural and spontaneous response of overflowing gratitude and humility.

Like everyone, I have had some significant areas of suffering in my life, and these have been hard, even excruciating, to live through. But I've discovered in such circumstances that when I yield to the Lord, I become more human, more compassionate, and I am often surprised by what I am able to do. I have realised that if we are to grow, we must always be challenged to move out of the shallows and embark into wider, deeper waters. And if we permit it, suffering can lead us into those deeper waters.

***

Reflecting like this on my personal visitation and encouragement of people awakens within me the awareness of the call of God in my life in a new way. For a very long time, I have been vividly aware of my definite call to be a good businessman and a man of deep faith, using my natural gifts to create a business that is dedicated to giving away as much as possible to the Lord's work in many places around the world. This is wonderful, but when I think about the deep satisfaction God has given me through all that, I am realising that it is not nearly as great as the delight and joy I have had through my relationships with so many beautiful people. For as I pay attention to the seeds of love for others and for evangelism present from my childhood and troubled teen years, I see how these have developed and multiplied as I've grown in faith and maturity and I am surprised to discover that this may have been an even greater call in my life than the work of Mission Enterprises.

This call to one-on-one ministry came more slowly and quietly, and so I did not realise so clearly before that this is what I have really been called to do. Recently, a friend referred to my love of people and my personal engagement with them as my "pastoral ministry," an expression of my "pastoral heart." This really made me laugh, because it appeared to elevate something so ordinary into a recognized ministry of the church, something sealed by ordination and a high vocational calling. Whereas I have always thought of it simply as something I loved!

But I have been wondering if my friend is recognizing something that I have missed. Perhaps a pastoral call *can* come to a layperson, who expresses that call within the context of ordinary life. Something about that resonates within me, and to my surprise, his words have found an unexpected home in me. They seem to describe what has happened in my life, though it has never occurred to me to think like that before, and it has touched me profoundly.

In many ways, I think of it as practising hospitality.[13] Through the beautiful ministry of hospitality, we participate in the Kingdom of God here on earth in very important ways. Our homes can become safe places for all kinds of people—from community leaders to those down on their luck. They can become places where people find encouragement for their lives, comfort in their sorrow, healing of body and spirit, courage to go on, relaxation or quiet friendship. Faith is born and strengthened as prayer is shared—not only in the one receiving hospitality, but also in the one offering it. Of course, for many reasons, it is not possible for everyone to open their homes in this way. But we can all begin to practise hospitality of the heart in small ways, which will grow as we foster hospitable attitudes of mind and heart by welcoming people as they are and providing a safe and healing listening space for them. As I have gone on with the Lord, I have tried to learn from him how to be more hospitable in this way—he who is always so generously hospitable to me.

Yesterday, I visited three or four people, which is a familiar pattern for most of my days now. These are just some of the people I feel drawn to visit and come alongside, to see how they are and to help them in a practical way or to pray with them if they wish. These brief visits are mutually encouraging, for when I leave, I feel enriched and blessed too. As long as I am able, I hope to continue in this quiet rhythm of visiting people. I love it, and I delight in seeing how the Lord gradually works miraculous changes within ordinary people and diverse circumstances through the silent, hidden presence of the Spirit.

Today, as I've been reflecting on all of these things, so many people have come into my mind, as if they're visiting me. Some have gone on with the Lord and some have not. Some I've lost touch with completely and I wonder how they are. Others I am still in touch with. I do love this part of my life—the people part. Thinking of them I find myself vividly experiencing them as I engaged with them in the past. But at the same time, I meet them in my mind now and enter the past through the reality of my greater age, experience and general maturity. I can touch past and present layers of this dimension of my life and it's been surprising to feel the flow of it within me—backward and forward over many years. This truly moving experience has underlined the richness of my relationships with a wide variety of people and the ways I have met God in them and been enriched by them. There have been so many, and I have appreciated all that I have received from them over the years.

Endnotes

1 In these words, Evelyn Underhill instructed those responsible for the spiritual formation of young people, insisting on the primary importance of their own experience of God if they wished to open others to a similar path. Her words resonate with Eugene's attitude to all his interactions with people. Cited by Joy Milos CSJ, "Evelyn Underhill, a Companion on Many Journeys," in *Traditions of Spiritual Guidance*, edited by Lavinia Byrne. London: Chapman, 1990, 135.

2 In many ways, Eugene's quiet unobtrusive "getting alongside" so many different people in a simple natural way reminded me of Father Joe, whose remarkable hidden ministry is described in the book by Tony Hendra. *Father Joe: The Man Who Saved my Soul*. Melbourne: Hamish Hamilton, 2004.

3 Olive was associated with Benwerrin from 1951 until her death in 1992, a place of retreat that provided sanctuary for hundreds of women and children. Mission Enterprises has been a major supporter of the Benwerrin ministry from 1981 to this present time, helping ensure its continuance beyond the deaths of both Olive and Eugene. For more information about Benwerrin see www.benwerrin.com.au.

4 Archbishop Fenelon, whom Eugene admired, writes concerning the care of others in this way: "One word from you will do more than thirty words spoken at an inappropriate moment...Always be alert to the time when God decides to give you a better opportunity, but do not anticipate that moment. This is the work of faith and the patience of saints. This work is carried out in the heart of the person who is trying to encourage the change of heart in his neighbour. The person who works in this way is continually dying to self as he tries to carry out God's will in the lives of other people." Archbishop Fenelon, *Christian Perfection*, edited by Halcyon Backhouse. London: Hodder and Stoughton, 1984, 74.

5 Madame Jeanne Guyon (1648–1717) observes, "As for the simple and unlearned, it is not true they are incapable of this interior relationship to Christ....Their humility, their simple trust in God, and their obedience make it easier for them to turn within and follow the Lord's Spirit. They are more qualified than most!" Quoted in *Experiencing the Depths of Jesus Christ* vol. 2 of Library of Spiritual Classics: Auburn, Maine: *Seed Sowers Christian Books* , 120.

6 The pastoral group to which Eugene refers here was in addition to the small healing group of which he was also a part. Both groups met weekly for teaching and prayer about their different areas of service and for the people involved. He greatly appreciated the learning and fellowship he received from these times.

7 The years when Eugene and Peter were visiting pastors around the State were full of lively debates in the denomination about the ordination of women, which had been going on for quite a long period. The first Baptist woman ordained in Australia was Marita Munro in 1978. Over the next decade, two more followed. Thus it is not surprising that during the period of Rev Peter Manton's ministry at Kew, there were no women ministers amongst those whom they visited in this way.

8 Peter was the minister of Kew Baptist Church from 1968–1985. He died suddenly of a heart attack when he was forty-eight. His death was a great shock to the church community, and Eugene, along with many others, grieved his loss deeply.

9 Julian of Norwich writes, "I saw God in a point, that is to say in my understanding, by which sight I saw that he is in all things. God is everything that is good, and the goodness that all things have, it is he." From *Revelations of Divine Love,* quoted in Karen Manton and Lynne Muir, *The Gift of Julian of Norwich* Mulgrave, Australia: John Garratt, 205), 36–37. And Hildegard of Bingen observes, "There is no creation that does not have a radiance." From *Meditations with Hildegard of Bingen.* Santa Fe, NM: Bear & Company, 1983, 24.

10 Eugene's experience is not unlike the one recorded by Thomas Merton in *Conjectures of a Guilty Bystander* New York: Image Books, Doubleday, 1966, 156–157: "In Louisville, at the corner of Fourth and Walnut, in the center of the shopping district, I was suddenly overwhelmed with the realization that I loved all those people, that they were mine and I theirs, that we could not be alien to one another even though we were total strangers. It was like waking from a dream of separateness...If only everybody could realize this! But it cannot be explained. There is no way of telling people that they are walking around shining like the sun." A bronze plaque in Louisville marks the spot where this happened to Merton on March 18, 1958 and notes how unusual it is for a mystical experience like this to be commemorated in such a way. The moment marked a turning point in Merton's life, leading him to pursue his monastic calling with a new engagement in social justice issues.

11 Ephesians 6:10–18.

12 Romans 5:5.

13 Romans 12:13.

VIII

You who sleep in my breast are not met with words, but in the emergence of life within life and of wisdom within wisdom. You are found in communion: Thou in me and I in Thee and Thou in them and they in me.

–Thomas Merton, *The Sign of Jonas*[1]

Joy unspeakable and full of glory

Whom having not seen, ye love; in whom, though now ye see him not, yet believing, ye rejoice with joy unspeakable and full of glory.

–1 Peter 1:8 KJV

My thoughts have returned to that confusing season in my teens, when my aching longing for assurance about my eternal salvation felt like a hopeless dream. Looking back, I can remember my anguish as I compared myself with other people in matters of faith and how that core of uncertainty radiated out and undermined my life and sense of well-being.

Then at the age of seventeen, when I was utterly desperate, I decided to trust God and to accept what is revealed through Jesus and the words of Scripture. This decision marked a major turning point in my life and became a kind of compass pointing me due north, helping me to steer my way through life's questions, controversies, failures and doubts. I learned not to get too tangled up in my swinging adolescent emotions or the theological, biblical and other debates swirling around me. After accepting in faith that my life was held in God, I began to live out of that as simply as I could, and the debilitating uncertainty about the state of my soul disappeared—and has never returned

When I look back at myself as that young Eugene, I can see quite poignantly how my faith has deepened and widened over a lifetime of practice, mistakes and failures. And so I have learned to become very cautious about saying too much about my more mature faith and experience, because I don't want to discourage those who are in different places in their journeys. But all that I have come to know of God has its origins in my teenage stance of surrender, which is reflected in the phrase, "meaning business with the Lord." Throughout my life, this simple, clarifying reminder has helped me realign myself around my deepest desire to surrender the intentions in both my inner and outer life to the Lord.

From the time of that decision of surrender, my longing to love God with my whole heart, soul, mind and strength became the focus of my prayer and my meditation. As a young adult, I formed the habit of spending twenty minutes or half an hour at the end of the day, sitting quietly in God's presence and letting my thoughts dwell on Jesus and how he reveals God to me. I found him to be very beautiful, and over time the Lord Jesus Christ became for me the altogether lovely one, whom these days I can seldom put out of my mind.

As I became more involved in business, I grew sharply aware of my daily need for God's wisdom, courage and guidance, particularly when I had to make decisions that seemed far beyond the scope of my minimal experience and formal education. Night after night, as we gathered for family worship, I would be overcome with emotion. Tears of gratitude and joy welled up as I gave thanks to the Lord for answered prayers—some even before I had asked. These precious experiences stayed with me in the daily routines of my life, when I had to get up the next morning to do my job, run the business, care for my family, tend church commitments, and engage with all the responsibilities and great opportunities of my life.

I don't know how to convey these times of awareness of the love and beauty of the Lord, which come and go when they will. But I remember reading about an incident in D. L. Moody's life,[2] when he was walking down the street in New York and was suddenly so overwhelmed by God's presence and love that he could barely keep moving and had to ask the Lord to stop. I understand such experiences, though I cannot make them happen, nor hold onto them indefinitely, but they remain with me and affect every part of my life. Even now as I recall them, I hear afresh that continuous cry of my heart for God. Sometimes, when I go to bed, I am so overwhelmed by the Lord's love that even though I am a good sleeper, I cannot go to sleep for sheer joy in the presence of God.[3] Sometimes I wish I had more of that, but what I have experienced has been beautiful.

As I think about the Lord's loving presence and his many gifts to me, I am struck by the reality that I am not attracted to the Lord because of the blessings I have received, but by who the Lord is himself. It's like falling in love with a girl. You don't fall in love with her because she's a good cook, or she plays tennis well, but you are attracted to her because you love her for herself, for who she is. As the Holy Spirit reveals the beauty of the Lord to me, the Lord himself is with me, and I can sense his presence and that in itself is enough.[4]

For many years now, I have made it my daily practice to go into my library in the evening and enjoy an hour or so of quiet reflection. I haven't had any dramatic experiences, such as seeing visions or hearing voices, but my deep and constant desire has been to know and love God. Gradually, over the span of many years, the Lord has revealed himself to me through my inner contemplation of him and his Word.[5] Now, anything that intrudes into this precious time of contemplation is a nuisance.

Over the years, my quiet, intentional sitting in the presence of God has become part of my meaning business with the Lord. Though my experience of what that means has grown and changed, it is the fruit of that early decision so many years ago.

After this period of reflection, I take up the Word to read. Sometimes, I turn to specific readings that I am studying at the time. Other times, I just pick up the Word and read wherever it opens. Whatever I read usually comes alive, and I feel the presence of God with me as he makes himself known through Scripture. Sometimes, I feel wooden and nothing comes leaping out at me, but most often the Word of God is active in me, and it becomes more precious as I continue to read.

I may just hear one word or phrase—"Our Father" or "He who has seen me has seen the Father"[6]—and then I enter another time of contemplation. Sometimes the words stay with me for days, and as I wonder about them, they gather life and energy in me, moving from my head to my soul, entering my spirit, where I am immersed in the beauty of the Lord and his Word.

After meditating on the Word, I am led naturally into prayer. When I was younger, I used to pray often about my needs and anxieties, which was natural. But for many years now, I find that I seldom pray for myself, because I am more concerned about the needs of others, and my focus is on praying for them in whatever way seems appropriate.

I usually begin my prayer with a review of the day in silence before the Lord. I was really surprised recently when I learned that this is a very old method of prayer, which is sometimes taught to those who want to learn more about how to pray. I have prayed this way naturally for years and found it very helpful. As I become conscious of all that God has done during that day—not just for me but for others—a spirit of gratitude comes into my heart. My whole spirit and body feel quickened and alive, surging with heightened awareness, and my heart overflows with praise and thanksgiving for the lavish goodness and kindness of God.

It is so easy to take things for granted—health, journeying mercies, family and friends, faith, food, clothes, shelter, freedom—if we don't stop every day to remember and give thanks to God. As I enter this time of thanksgiving, I see a whole train of things—a person's kindness, the way a conversation opened up, how someone I needed turned up during the day—and I realize that I would not have registered any of this if I had not allowed the day to pass before me in this quiet, prayerful way. Every day, I endeavour to give thanks for such mercies. This practice has made me more aware of those who lack basic human necessities, and it has moved me to take action wherever I can.

Of course, everything in my life wasn't lovely all the time. I had many problems in the business and many tough times personally, but through all these difficulties, I was conscious of the Lord working with me to overcome them. My awareness of the Lord's faithfulness in spite of my inadequacies brought me to tears repeatedly and nurtured my faith in God as a worker of miracles.[7] God is infinitely more beautiful than we can imagine—and certainly more ready to give to us than we are to receive.

After reflecting on the day and responding with praise and thanksgiving, I pray for those who have asked for prayer, or for whom I am concerned, or whom the Lord lays on my heart in a special way. As I pray for each person the Lord puts on my heart, I am filled with unspeakable joy, because I am being invited to be involved in the mysterious work of God in the heart of another person. I am drawn deeply into the love of God as I pray. Though he can do all things without my prayer, he wants me and others who are praying for this person to be involved in their guidance or in their physical, mental or spiritual healing. Sometimes, as I am drawn deeper into prayer for a person, I know how God is inviting me to pray. At other times, I am uncertain, and so I ask the Lord to guide me as I pray, trusting the Spirit[8] to take the deep longing of my heart for this person's well-being and to gather it into God in ways that are beyond my intellectual comprehension. As I am immersed in this prayer, I know without any shadow of a doubt that God is working faithfully in this person's heart and will answer the prayer in some way. Sometimes I discover that purpose—and sometimes I don't.

During these evening times of contemplation, meditation upon Scripture and prayer, I have grown in my trust of God, and my awareness of his presence over the years has become more acute. I have come to experience God himself as distinct from just thinking about him,[9] and I have discovered that I can enter this awareness at any time—driving the car, in a meeting, anywhere. Nowadays, after years of practice, this way of prayer has become habitual.[10] In this sense, I am praying continually, which I think is what the apostle Paul meant when he said, "pray without ceasing."[11] To evoke the sense of the Lord's presence with me in this way is impossible to convey in words, but I experience a beautiful naturalness and a feeling of being at home, as if my whole being is gathered into love.

Sometimes I have to miss my evening times with the Lord for some reason, such as illness, or not getting home until midnight when I'm very tired. Then I simply say to the Lord, "I'm weary and tired, I love you, I praise you," and get quickly into bed. It's not good to become legalistic about it, or to assume that I'll have a bad day tomorrow because I missed my hour of prayer today. God is not that kind of heavenly Father.[12] But I have benefitted so much from practising these habits of prayer, and I couldn't go for more than two or three days without this time. I wouldn't be me. Some people tell me they pray continually and don't have a set time. Others tell me they might not pray for a week, or read the Word for days. But I don't see how they can live the Christian life without consistent, intentional times of prayer and meditation.

I wish that everyone had the same experience of God's overwhelming love and goodness. I don't understand why I have been so blessed in this way. I can understand the apostle Paul when he wrote to the church in Rome and said that he so longed for them to know God in Christ that he would be willing to lose his own salvation in order for them to know the Lord.[13] He is trying to explain how deeply he cared for them. I feel the same about many people. I care so deeply for them that I yearn for them to know the Lord—and this is both painful and hopeful at the same time. Sometimes, I say to myself that it would be far better if I were blotted out if that meant that others would enter into this close bond with God.

***

In my desire to mean business with the Lord, I realised the importance of making my inner sense of God become a practical down-to-earth part of how I lived. Of course this is commonsense. When I sense God awakening my mind, heart or spirit, or drawing me to move beyond where I am, then I have to start acting on that insight in a practical way in my ordinary life if

I want it to develop. If I don't, I will come to a full-stop in this area, and my heart will likely grow harder, and I will be less able to hear the invitations of the Spirit. In this way, there's no standing still—we're either going forward into living new insights from God, or we are going backwards.[14] This has been borne out in what I've seen of life and people and what I have discovered in my own life. When we are obedient to each new understanding we receive, we will be stretched, and we will change and grow.

For example, if I long to pray more deeply or more in tune with God's Spirit, then I can only move out of my present knowledge by actually praying. If I just talk about prayer with others, or read books on prayer, or attend retreats and seminars on prayer, I will only learn in a theoretical way. I'm certainly not saying that seminars, discussions and books about prayer are irrelevant or useless, but they alone will not teach me to pray. For the only way to learn how to pray is to pray. We often make prayer complicated and dreary, but really it is a bit like breathing. We simply need to be natural and honest as we sit frequently in the beautiful presence of God, open to receive—often without saying anything, but present with the longing to be with him. [15]

This decision to mean business with the Lord in how I respond to the insights of the Spirit requires simple, ordinary faithfulness, where I commit to do whatever God is stirring me to do—both when the sun is shining and when I can't see it for the low black clouds that encircle me. And when for some reason I stop doing this, I have found it best simply to start again. For through all the ups and downs of my life, there has always been a calling to love, a calling to return, and an abundance of forgiveness. I see this as another aspect of obedience, to saying yes to God's longing for communion with us and for our communion with one another.

At the moment, I am reading Jeremiah and Lamentations and other parts of the Old Testament, and I am very touched by the Lord's extreme longing and desire for the Jewish people to know him and love him and keep his ways. This reminds me of the longing that Jesus expresses in his prayers to the Father in John's Gospel and his tremendous desire to draw us into a deep communion of love with him and each other.[16]

As I dwell on God's longing to be in loving relationship with us, I am overwhelmed by the fact that God is so gracious and mindful of us. In the busy routines of life, it is easy to become numb to God's astounding desire for deep communion with us.[17] But if we open ourselves to God's desire for us in tiny ways, he will draw our deepest longings toward himself like a magnet. As we live out of this awareness, we will move away from seeing God as a Father Christmas figure to be used and manipulated for our own desires, and we will be drawn into a love relationship that starts to transform us to live in God's ways. The Lord longs to give us far more than we are able to imagine, for God is far more willing to give than we are to receive.[18] But as the psalmist says, we are dust,[19] and our capacity to understand the Lord's abundant generosity is limited because we are finite. We see through a glass, darkly.

My greatest gift has been the experience of God himself—not any particular work he has given me to do or any special blessings.[20] Though I'm thankful that God has been able to use me through the business and the work of Mission Enterprises, my own relationship with the Lord surpasses everything. It never ceases to surprise me that God has poured out his love and goodness upon me in such a lavish and overwhelming way, giving me—an ordinary, unworthy servant—such tremendous joy and peace. It's as if I've just done some normal little thing, such as pick up an old lady's handbag for her in the street when she dropped it, and then she takes me home, sends me $1,000 and arranges a trip to Europe for me. And I only picked up her handbag!

The closer my relationship with God becomes, the more joy I experience. I resonate with the psalmist who writes, "In Thy presence there is fullness of joy and at thy right hand there are pleasures forevermore."[21] However, though my experience of tremendous joy is very real, I want to emphasise that it is not the main thing for me. Most of the time, I sense God's peace or the Lord's quiet presence without any tumultuous emotion. I don't feel the need for great mountain-top experiences, and I see danger in chasing after them for their own sake. The most important thing by far is to seek the Lord for himself with my whole heart—and to mean business about it. My experiences of joy unspeakable and full of glory come out of obeying what I believe is God's will as simply and faithfully as I can.[22]

But we often spend so much time worrying about discerning God's will for us in the complex decisions of life that we overlook the fact that in most of our ordinary daily interactions with people, God has made his will very clear. So we can start by simply deciding to get on with practising these down-to-earth acts of obedience. For example, we are told, "as we have opportunity, let us do good to all people," and we can practise this in the little things that come across our paths every day. When we are told, "Let us therefore no longer pass judgement on one another," and "be forgiving,"[23] we can become aware every day of the numerous opportunities we are given to practice such simple acts of obedience to God.[24]

But when I become careless or tired or struggle with heavy problems, it is hard to practise these simple acts of obedience. When this happens, it is easy for me to get hooked in a downward spiral of despondency and self-condemnation. But I have learned that this is very foolish, for when I begin to drown in remorse and guilt, my focus shifts to myself and my failures, and this cripples my communion with the Lord. Therefore, as soon as the Holy Spirit makes me aware of my unkind spirit, judgemental attitudes or lack of awareness, I have learned that it is better to return swiftly to the Lord with my disappointment in myself and to confess my actions and my sorrow for any harm I have caused.

For I have come to realize that the Lord is not waiting with a great big hammer to berate me, but rather to accept, love, encourage me and send me out into life again—more compassionate and gracious. Sometimes, the Holy Spirit nudges me in the right direction through the concern of another person. Because of this, I have learned to appreciate it when a friend gently suggests, "Eugene, I think you're not on the right track here," or "Eugene, I feel that this is not right in your life."

***

So I'm learning to trust in the slow work of God in myself and other people. Obedience and transparent honesty are essential in nurturing a loving communion with God—and the outcome of our sincere repentance will always bear the fruit of the Holy Spirit and return us to that deeper communion. The closer I stay to the Lord, in the sense of this communion, the freer I become internally, and this inner freedom naturally flows into my everyday life in simple ways. It is the fruit of the indwelling Spirit spoken of in Scripture: "Now the Lord is the Spirit and where the Spirit of the Lord is, there is freedom."[25]

For example, when I am criticised, I don't get as devastated and upset as I used to, nor am I so easily offended, because I feel very secure in the

Lord's love and acceptance of me. Because of this inner resilience, I am able to hold criticism more lightly and consider whether it is true or not, or whether God is speaking to me through it. If he is, then I can receive it and act on it, which frees me even more. If it is not true, I can let it go instead of fretting so much about it.

Another characteristic of this interior freedom is that I no longer need to put on such a protective facade to shield my wounds and vulnerability. I have become more accepting of myself because every day I experience the loving acceptance of God, which gives me an inner confidence and frees me from the crippling fear of rejection, which plagued me through my teens and early adult years. There is a sense of lightness, and I am not so burdened and anxious as I once was.

I have also become far more accepting of other people as they are—less biased and judgemental. I notice this in many different ways. One of these is in my upbringing in the conservative evangelical tradition, where I remain. I continue to be grateful for the many faithful people who have prayed for me, taught me, challenged me and encouraged me in this tradition. But like any other tradition, it has its prejudices that are equated with the will of God. I have found that the more I am able to remain in loving communion with God, the more I am set free from some of these prejudices, which are not really from God, but rather from our human need to control things— even God at times—so we feel a bit safer. I think we need to be delivered from this sort of thing.

It is such a joy when we find beautiful fellowship with people from other Christian traditions and meet the Lord in them, too. I have found that when I am in communion with the Lord, I am in communion with all parts of the Church because the Lord is. There is great freedom in this for me.[26] Although complete freedom in Christ will take a life-time, as I look back through the years, I can at least see that I am moving in that direction!

When I consider the years since I was a little boy and see how the Lord has drawn me to himself, helped me and carried me, I am filled with love and gratitude. Because I am continually conscious of his presence now, I never cease communing with him, and so I am always conscious of how good God is in everything, and my heart overflows with gratitude. This in turn makes me more generous in my spirit and attitude towards others— especially if I have problems with them.

Yet I know well how easy it is to harden my heart towards God, certain people, ideas, cultures and so on. I notice that sometimes I do this because I'm trying to protect myself from recurring past hurt and I'm trying to heal. But other times, it's because I'm so familiar with something I've heard often, and so I become a bit bored, and I put up barriers of resistance and dismiss it. This can happen with familiar aspects of the Gospel when I think, "I know all that!" and so miss out on what God has to say to me. A lot of people who have been brought up in the church feel this way. For this reason, the biblical picture of the hard heart and the soft heart helps me pay attention to the way I hear all sorts of things—not just religious ones.[27]

I am moved by God's promise to give a tender heart, because at times I have felt my own heart softened towards some person or around some issue, and I know that God awakened compassion in me and helped me to become more open and to listen more carefully. This is the Holy Spirit working in my heart to make it soft and tender. It does not necessarily mean that I become gullible, although it does mean that I become more vulnerable to inner and outer pain—my own and other people's. For a soft and compassionate heart is a vulnerable heart.

Yet strangely, in my own experience in the business world, I sometimes had dealings with people who were devious schemers and had no hesitation in taking other people down, particularly those who were as devious and cunning as themselves. Some would take their own grandmother down, and yet would not do that to someone they perceived as honest and open. Because I was seen as a truthful bloke and had a reputation in the industry that my nay was nay and my yes was yes, they didn't seem to have the heart to use me in this way. So in those instances, it seemed that my honesty and simple vulnerability protected me in a way that sometimes surprised and moved me.

***

Because I feel deeply loved and accepted by God, I have learned to accept and love myself and others more freely, and this has deepened my inner tranquillity and calm. I think this is partly what is meant by the words, "a sabbath rest still remains for the people of God."[28] This rest is not for a future heaven, but for now, here in this world. Such rest does not mean loafing, for there is plenty of work to be done! But as we endure trials and tribulations, an inner peace will remain. And though the surface of our lives may be turbulent, underneath this there will be restfulness.

In this restfulness, I realise that the Lord is taking me on, and I know without a shadow of doubt that he is working for good in my life.[29] To my great surprise, I find that I am able to attend to the commitments, responsibilities and challenges of my life without the old familiar strain and stress of self-effort. As I cooperate with God in prayer and action and allow the Spirit to work through me, remaining open to how he stirs my interactions with others and my planning for the business, I experience this rest.[30]

But there is another way that I experience this rest amidst turbulence. Two nights ago, my daughter came to see me, and she told me about a couple of women she had been helping and about whom she was very concerned. As I listened, I became overwhelmed with their needs and with the needs of many others. I felt so burdened that I knelt down and prayed, and this was both hard and easy. Even though I was in absolute communion with the Lord and knew that there was nothing between us, I felt very sad as I carried this burden.[31] Perhaps this is what Jesus meant when he said his burden was light.[32]

I have an enormous list of people for whom I feel called to pray, and now that I am living alone, I keep it on my kitchen table night and day, so that whenever I sit at the table, I pray for them. This burden comes upon me as I commune with the Lord—and I feel its weight precisely because of my communion with him. In some ways, the closer I come to the Lord, the more of these burdens I carry—and this is similar to my deep concern for some of the people in my life who do not know the Lord. When the Lord puts them on my heart, I sometimes weep for them, but in the Lord's presence, I also feel joy and freedom. Such prayer is burdensome and costly, yet easy at the same time. When I am working hard in this light way, I am often conscious of the Lord's smile upon me. This is beautiful, like a gentle blessing covering me. This is part of the restfulness. I am put into a restful place.[33]

***

There is another burden I carry, which I find almost unbearable, and this is the doctrine of eternal torment for the unconverted. I know many others have struggled with this.[34] I certainly think that sin and rebellion against God have inevitable consequences in our lives, but to say that the majority of humanity will suffer terrible torment for eternity dishonours and maligns the loving character of God revealed in Jesus, with whom I have experienced such deep and loving communion over so many years.

We cannot comprehend eternity, but here is an image to consider. At the centre of our continent, in the vast desert, is the iconic rock Uluru,[35] a gigantic monolith that is 1,150 feet high and five miles around its base, sacred to the Indigenous people and of huge symbolic significance to most Australians. If a sparrow came along once in a million years and scraped its beak on the rock, the time it would take to wear it down to the ground is just the start of eternity. I am totally unable to accept the idea that anyone thinks that God would condemn people to eternal torture. Such an understanding of the nature of God causes me the most dreadful anguish and sorrow.

The doctrine of eternal damnation is a stumbling block to non-Christians, and it is particularly offensive to sensitive, thoughtful and intelligent people. Young people have told me that they are leaving the faith because they cannot contemplate this doctrine with integrity. Yet some people say that if you don't believe the doctrine of eternal torment, then you won't have any incentive to convert people! Still others say that God has ordained that you and I will be converted, but that most others will be consigned to hell forever. Preaching such terrible doctrine to people of other faiths and beliefs is completely outrageous and destructive. I cannot speak with integrity about my communion with God over most of my life without speaking of this matter, for it is precisely because of this communion that I carry this dreadful burden of sorrow for God.

Speaking as I have about such a controversial topic reminds me of how important it is to allow one another the space to be vulnerable and transparent. We need to create safe places where we can be respected and accepted for who we are without fearing judgement or rejection. I am clearer now about how I suffer from these burdens precisely because of my communion with the Lord and my sense of who he is, even though there is so much I don't know or understand clearly. These burdens are the fruit of the prayer I have been praying nearly all of my life: "that I may know him and the power of his resurrection and the fellowship of his suffering."[36] I believe that the more we long to know God, if we mean business about it, the more we will enter into both the suffering and resurrection of Jesus.

***

In my experience, faith is not just about going to church, or singing hymns and happy choruses, or waving your arms in the air. We worship God through our inner attitudes and our outer service to others.[37] Praying for someone is very important, but if I can help that person in a practical way and don't, my prayers count for nothing because God has given me the ability to help them and I don't.[38] We are to be as concerned for the welfare of others as we are for ourselves, including those who despitefully use us. When I get down to the nitty gritty difficulty of doing this, I am worshipping God. Worship in church is, of course, part of true worship, but what I do and who I am after I leave the sanctuary is my worship in everyday life. The two cannot be separated.

There are burdens to be carried, and anyone who means business with the Lord will have some of these to carry. They may not be about hell, but simply about the state of the world we live in. We can't be radiant when we know of the injustice and suffering in the world. We must shoulder these burdens, this suffering with God[39] and live out our faith in ordinary life. Thinking about this, I have meditated on the Lord's prayer for many hours at a time on and off over the years, and I often find myself weeping at the love of God for all of us.

There are many things I do not understand—so many tragedies, so much suffering, and so many unanswered questions—but one thing I do know is that God is love.[40] This teaching is so familiar that it can become meaningless—an idea that we assent to in a general sort of way, but which lacks the power of genuine lived experience. Love is not an attribute of God, but who God is. All the other characteristics of God—mercy, justice, compassion, beauty, holiness, goodness—are enfolded in the Love *who is God*.

This awareness has grown very deep in me over many years, but if we want to experience more of who God is—and not only learn about him in theory—then we must mean business with him and embark on the adventure of loving him. This is summed up in the great commandment: "you will love the Lord your God with all your heart and with all your soul and with all your mind and with all your strength and your neighbour as yourself."[41] This commandment is full of invitation and hope when it is also heard as a promise to those who set out, often hesitantly, on this way.

My longing to know God more has continued to grow ever since I seriously committed myself to the journey of learning to love God and other people in my ordinary everyday living. Of course, I am still a beginner, and I have made many mistakes, detours and struggles like everyone else. But as I have followed this way to the best of my ability, I *have* come to know and love God more and I know this is just the beginning of all that is yet to come. I think this is the way Jesus lived as well—and he invites us to follow him.

This way is not always easy, but we're on safe ground here. Never mind all the things we don't know. Let us get on with living this, which we *do* know.

Endnotes

1 Thomas Merton, *The Sign of Jonas* cited in *Thomas Merton, Spiritual Master: Essential Writings*. Mahwah, NJ: Paulist, 1992, 119

2 Famous nineteenth-century American evangelist.

3 In *Reality of the Spiritual World* (1944; reprint, London: Quaker Home Service, 1996, 28), Thomas Kelly writes, "One may have said all one's life, God is love. But there is an experience of the love of God which, when it comes upon us, and enfolds us, and bathes us, and warms us, is so utterly new that we can hardly identify it with the old phrase, God is love. Can this be the love of God, this burning, tender, wooing, wounding pain of love that pierces the marrow of my bones." Eugene knew and often expressed this kind of experience.

4 Similar sentiments are expressed by St. Teresa of Avila: "who God possesseth, in nothing is wanting; alone God sufficeth." Quoted in "Midday Office," *Celtic Daily Prayer*, The Northumbia Community London: Harper and Collins, 2005, 29. Julian of Norwich: "God of your goodness give me your self, for you are enough for me...if I ask anything that is less, ever I am wanting...only in you I have all." From *Revelations of Divine Love*, as quoted in Karen Manton, *The Gift of Julian of Norwich*, 96. St. Augustine: "Give me Thine own self, without which, though Thou shouldest give me all that ever Thou hast made, yet could not my desires be satisfied." Quoted in *Great Souls at Prayer*, compiled by Mary W. Tileston, 1898; reprint, London: Allenson & Co. Ltd., 1946, 108.

5 A well-known statement attributed to St. Augustine speaks of the experience of falling in love with God, which is wonderfully reminiscent of Eugene's conversations with me: "To fall in love with God is the greatest romance; to seek him the greatest adventure; to find him the greatest human achievement." Similarly, the following sentiment is attributed to Soren Kierkegaard: "Just as in earthly life lovers long for the moment when they are able to breathe forth their love for each other, to let their souls blend in a soft whisper, so the mystic longs for the moment when in prayer he can, as it were, creep into God."

6 Matthew 6:9; John 14:9.

7 "I am the ground of thy praying—/ first, it is my will that thou have something,/ and next I make thee to want it,/ and afterwards I cause thee to pray for it./ If thou prayest for it,/ How then could it be that thou wouldst not get what thou asked for?" Julian of Norwich, *Showings*. Translated by John-Julian, OJN, in *Love's Trinity, A Companion to Julian of Norwich*. Collegeville, MN: Liturgical Press, 2009, 146.

8 Romans 8:26–27.

9 Eugene's intentional habit of spending time each evening, quietly loving God before anything else, matured into this "acute sense of God himself as distinct from thinking about him." This calls to mind the words of the anonymous fourteenth-century author of *The Cloud of Unknowing*: "He can certainly be loved, but not thought, He can be taken and held by love but not by thought." See Austin Cooper, *The Cloud: Reflections on Selected Texts*. Homebush NSW: St. Paul, 1989, 85. This communion of love and Eugene's desire to live in obedience to this love shaped the development of his inner attitudes and outer actions.

10 Thomas Kelly stresses: "Within us is a meeting place with God...There is a way of living in prayer at the same time that one is busy with the outward affairs of daily life. This practice of continuous prayer in the presence of God involves developing the habit of carrying on the mental life at two levels. At one level we are immersed in this world of time, of daily affairs. At the same time, but at a deeper level of our minds, we are in active relation with the Eternal Life" *Reality of the Spiritual World* 1944; reprint, London: Quaker Home Service, 1996, 34–35. Kelly and Eugene both spoke of this mode of prayer frequently and naturally, elaborating on it, as do many others whose communion with God becomes continuous.

11 1 Thessalonians 5:17.

12 Eugene's confidence in the compassionate love of God when he misses prayer for reasons of tiredness is reminiscent of Brother Lawrence's stance on falling asleep while praying: "Those who have the gale of the Holy Spirit go forward even in sleep." From *The Practice of the Presence of God*, quoted in Robert Llewelyn, *With Pity Not With Blame*. Norwich, UK: Canterbury Press, 2013, 90. Llewelyn adds: "sleep is an important though much overlooked way in which the Holy Spirit completes his work in us."

13 Romans 9:2–3.

14 "If you do not strive for the virtues and practice them you will always be dwarfs. And, please God, it will only be a matter of not growing, for you already know that whoever does not increase decreases. I hold that love, where present, cannot possibly be content with remaining always the same." From *The Collected Works of St Teresa of Avila*, vol. 2, The Interior Castle Washington, D.C.: ICS, 1980, 447. Consider also, "Genuine goodness is a matter of habitually acting and responding appropriately in each situation, as it arises, moved always by the desire to please God." *The Cloud of Unknowing*. Translated by W. Johnston. Garden City, NY: Image 1973, 64.

15 Compare with the following from *The Cloud of Unknowing*: "one loving blind desire for God alone is more valuable in itself, more pleasing to God...more beneficial to your own growth...than anything else you could do." *The Cloud of Unknowing*. Translated by W. Johnston. Garden City, NY: Image 1973, 60.

16 John 17:20–23.

17 Eugene lived with wonder about his awareness of God's deep desire for us, and this experience is frequently referred to in mystical literature. Compare with these words from Meister Eckhart c1260–1328): "God is foolishly in love with us. It seems he has forgotten heaven and earth and all his happiness and deity; his entire business seems to be with me alone, to give me everything to comfort me; he gives it to me suddenly, he gives it to me wholly, he gives it to me perfect, he gives it all the time and he gives it to all creatures" as

cited in Douglas Steer, *Together in Solitude*, New York: Crossroads, 1985, 136. Frank Laubach (1884–1970) echoes this insatiable love in *Letters by a Modern Mystic* first published in the USA by the Student Volunteer Movement, fifth impression 1957, 24. "Grant Me the shared joy of being loved by you. For I too, by my very nature, am hungry with an insatiable hunger for the love of all of you...so while we love each other, child, My share is as keen as yours."

18 Eugene reiterated this emphatically many times during our discussions, and it resonates with many from the mystical tradition, cf. Meister Eckhart: "God is found to act, to pour himself into thee as soon as ever he shall find thee ready...He longs for thee a thousand-fold more urgently than thou for him." Steer, *Together in Solitude*, 137. Frank Laubach , *Letters*: "There is...so much more in Him than He can give us, because we are so sleepy and so pitifully small" 24, "I know that God is love hungry" 25.

19 Psalm 103:14.

20 Meister Eckhart writes, "To seek nothing and to set out only for God himself is to discover God who gives the seeker all that is in his divine heart." Quoted in Charles R. Ringma. *Hear the Ancient Wisdom*, Eugene, OR: Cascade, 2013, 183.

21 Psalm 16:11.

22 Cf. St. Teresa of Avila: "The highest perfection does not consist in interior joys, nor in sublime raptures, nor in visions, nor in having the gift of prophecy, but in bringing our will into such conformity with the will of God, that whatever we know He desires, that also shall we desire with our whole affection." Quoted in Douglas Steer, *Together in Solitude*, 199).

23 Galatians 6:10; Romans 14:13; Ephesians 4:32.

24 *The Cloud of Unknowing* comments in a similar practical way, "genuine goodness is a matter of habit, acting and responding appropriately in each situation as it arises, moved always by the desire to please God." As quoted in Charles Ringma, *Hear the Ancient Wisdom*, Eugene, OR: Cascade, 2013, 137.

25 2 Corinthians 3:17.

26 Eugene grew up in a time when denominational boundaries were more rigid than they generally are today. It is significant that this wide-hearted response grew out of his prayer and communion with God.

27 "A new heart I will give you, and a new spirit I will put within you; and I will remove from your body the heart of stone and give you a heart of flesh." Ezekiel 36:26 (NRSV). The Quakers frequently speak of the tendering of the heart, which is the fruit of the Holy Spirit's indwelling presence in a believer. Eugene was very open to this action of God in himself and to returning to the communion which produced this heart when he had moved away from it. St. Teresa of Avila in her Life offers evidence of a tender heart as one of the "jewels" of true mystical experience as distinct from false mystical experiences: "the soul that has experienced this prayer and this union is left with a very great tenderness of such a kind that it would gladly become consumed not with pain but in tears of joy." Cited in Douglas Steer, *Together in Solitude*, 147.

28 Hebrews 4:9 NRSV.

29 "Rest. Rest. Rest in God's love. The only work you are required now to do is to give your most intense attention to His still, small voice within." Attributed to Madame Jeanne Guyon

(1648–1717).

30 "I feel simply carried along each hour, doing my part in a plan which is far beyond myself. The sense of co-operation with God in little things is what so astonishes me...The sense of being led by an unseen hand which takes mine while another hand reaches ahead and prepares the way, grows upon me daily" Laubach, *Letters*, 14–15).

31 "That there are trials and sufferings and that at the same time, the soul is in peace is a very difficult thing to explain." St Teresa of Avila, *The Interior Castle* , 437.

32 Matthew 11:30.

33 "Come to me, all you that are weary and are carrying heavy burdens and I will give you rest" Matthew 11:28 (NRSV).

34 Julian of Norwich is one such person. The following words indicate the struggle she had with the doctrine of eternal punishment and the way it conflicted with her own revelations of the Passion of Christ and his repeated assurances that 'all will be well': "One article of our faith is that many creatures will be...eternally condemned to hell...And all this being so, it seemed impossible to me that every kind of thing should be well, as our Lord revealed at this time." He answered her: "What is impossible to you is not impossible to me. I shall preserve my word in everything, and I shall make everything well." "And in this I was taught by the grace of God that I ought to keep myself steadfastly in the faith, as I had understood before, and that at the same time I should stand firm and believe that every kind of thing will be well, as our Lord revealed at that same time." From Julian of Norwich, *Revelations of Divine Love*, in Kerrie Hide: *Gifted Origins to Graced Fulfillment: The Soteriology of Julian of Norwich* Collegeville, MN: Liturgical Press, 2001, 185, 187.

35 Also at times called Ayers Rock.

36 Philippians 3:10.

37 Romans 12:1–2.

38 James 2:14–17.

39 In *The Silent Cry*, 140, Dorothee Soelle points to the suffering which arises from the mystical experience of the oneness and wholeness at the heart of life. This heightens the awareness of the unrelenting fragmentation and brokenness of life. "Finding God fragmented into rich and poor, top and bottom, sick and well, weak and mighty: that's the mystic's suffering." This suffering is also the source of the mystics' energy for resistance to injustice, oppression and other forms of suffering in the world. Such suffering is behind Eugene's anguish about the understanding of God behind the doctrine of eternal damnation. In a related awareness, note: Dietrich Bonhoeffer: "Christians stand with God in God's suffering" quoted in *The Silent Cry*, 152). Thomas Kelly: "He [God] lays on us new burdens. He sensitizes us in new areas toward God and toward men" *Reality of the Spiritual World*, 50. Attributed to St John of the Cross: "the suffering for the neighbour grows the more as the soul unites itself through love of God."

40 1 John 4:8.

41 Luke 10:25–28.

VIII

A saint is a person who practises the keystone virtue of humility... This man is one of those rare, rare creatures. Gentleness and goodness come off him like aftershave.

—Tony Hendra, *Father Joe: the Man who Saved my Soul*[1]

Epilogue

I have set before you an open door.

–Revelation 3:8 NRSV

Eugene shortly before his death in 2010 - courtesy of The Age, Angel Wylie/Fairfax Syndication

After our initial conversations, Eugene lived another twenty-one years. His life continued to be full, creative, kind, and faithful. He did not believe in retirement unless health and mental inability enforced it. In his later years, he retained his keen mind, deep faith and sense of humour even as he became increasingly frail and struggled with the challenges of old age. He enjoyed engaging in his regular pastoral visitation until he was in his nineties and maintained an active role in the ongoing development of Mission Enterprises until his death.

Following the sale of the transport business to Mayne Nicholas in 1986 and their establishment of Veith Parceline in 1988, Mission Enterprises became primarily an investment company, which continued to prosper and give away millions of dollars in profits to projects in Australia and overseas. Then in 2008, Eugene, in collaboration with the Mission Enterprises Board, established the Entrust Foundation, which is run by Mission Enterprises.[2] This allows many more people to be directly involved in his vision by becoming donors to a variety of projects around the world that continue to bless and heal people. They are able to participate in the expertise and partnerships built up over many years by Mission Enterprises, knowing that the foundation ensures that 100 percent of all donations is used for the project or cause selected by the donor. This is possible because of Eugene's foresight and generosity and the capital he left invested for this purpose, which—along with some corporate sponsorship—covers all the administrative and project selection costs. This initiative has allowed Mission Enterprises to multiply the effectiveness of its support by 200 percent—a figure that continues to rise.

In death as well as life, Eugene has ensured that the business he established as a shy, hesitant teenager will continue to support the Lord's work around the world. The impossible dream of his childhood continues to unfold against all the odds which were in his mind when he woke up and said to himself: "I don't believe it. That will never happen!"

* * *

After listening to Eugene tell his story and allowing it to simmer in me for a long time, my experience of finally writing it has been multilayered, ranging from the mundane and ordinary to the surprising and extraordinary. A twentieth-century Aussie man, Eugene began his life in a rural area in a close-knit, loving, conservative-evangelical family that struggled with poverty and illness. This family planted seeds of faith in him. The child with the grand name became a humble man who was extremely practical in his engagement with the ordinary daily round of his life and his longing to incarnate his love of God there. He knew the experience of "being called by name" by the God who wooed him from an early age. His experience of God and the language he used to describe it is often reminiscent of the Christian mystical tradition.

Dorothee Soelle notes, "The history of mysticism is a history of love for God."[3] I think it is possible to understand Eugene as one of those ordinary hidden mystics whom Dorothy Soelle acknowledges in *The Silent Cry: Mysticism and Resistance,* when she voices her concern to "democratize mysticism" and open the door to the mystic sensibility which is in all of us. More than one theologian has remarked that the Christians of the future will be mystics. My hunch is that they have always been present and that they are among us today, quietly unobtrusive, but secure in the unfathomable love of God they know enfolds everything and out of which they live and work in large and small ways for the rule of God in our time. In the general rush of daily life, people seldom talk of their experience of God at this deep and intimate level, but in the right context and at the right time, some do. When such experiences of God are articulated, it is a deep privilege to listen in and to recognise that we are on holy ground.

In his reflections, Eugene has invited us to listen to the story of his life as if from the comfort of an armchair drawn up beside him. We have heard him talk of the faithful love that enfolded and sustained him through both good and hard times. He has told us about the courteous Lord's gentle, strong and compassionate presence as a guide through periods of light and darkness. We have listened to him speak of the Spirit of truth, who called him back to himself and to God when he stepped out of line, filling him with a tender and wise heart. He has told us about the gracious One who restored his spirit and renewed his zest for life when he was at a low ebb. We have sat beside him when he struggled to describe his own experience of the baffling mystery at the heart things—the divine beauty, the altogether lovely one. As we have listened, we may have encountered the humble God, stooping to dwell within a fragile mortal and bringing the divine to life in him.

Eugene's response to the divine presence is like a tree responding to the wind blowing through its leaves and branches in all the different seasons of life. The movement of the compassionate God, who is with us and for us, is felt in his engagements with the events and people he encountered during his long life of struggle and joy. His amazement of the God whom he experienced as unspeakable joy, full of glory, is conveyed in his reverent attempts to capture the wonder of the divine presence in words. As Eugene matured, he lived with an habitual awareness of God, maintaining both depth and balance between his inner and outer life as he sought to incarnate all he was learning through his communion with God into the daily affairs of his life. His deep love for and knowledge of God was formed through prayer and obedience.

The heritage of his faith continues to touch and bless hundreds today who never knew him personally, and this wide legacy will flow into the future, bringing life and hope to others yet to be born. This comes not only through the ministries of the business he established, but also through the diverse relationships of his daily life—family, friends, business colleagues, and the people he visited and prayed with.[4] It continues in those who awakened to God or were healed through his care; those he gently admonished or helped in practical ways and those he touched as a counsellor and advisor in evangelistic missions. Finally there are the hundreds he influenced during his seventy faithful years, many of these as a deacon, with Kew Baptist Church.

He was a man of simple yet deep faith, of spontaneous laughter and tears, whose life was marked by compassion and humility. Generous in spirit, he was also vulnerable and aware of his weaknesses and mistakes. Though he was "just an ordinary bloke," there was always the sense that something deeply extraordinary was happening as he engaged with the divine in the nitty gritty of his daily life. No one was more surprised than Eugene about the way his life unfolded and he would undoubtedly say that all this has happened "because the Lord took me on".

Endnotes

1 Tony Hendra, *Father Joe: The man Who saved My Soul*, 4.

2 For more information, see www.entrust.org.au and associated links. Richard Beaumont, who had joined the Mission Enterprises Board in 2001, was appointed part-time CEO in 2008, a position that became full-time in 2011, which he still holds in 2016.

3 Dorothee Soelle, *The Silent Cry*, 2.

4 The Eugene Veith meditation room in the rebuilt El Kanah guesthouse in Marysville is one contemporary embodiment of this.

Acknowledgments

I wish to thank members from Eugene's family, particularly Adele and David, for their help with information and photos and for their encouragement. I appreciate too, the support I have received from Stuart Brown, Richard Beaumont and Dirk Bakker, who with their long involvement in Mission Enterprises and the Entrust foundation have been very helpful clarifying matters concerning the business and its historical development and present day operation. Karen Hollenbeck-Wuest has been a skilful editor who understood the spirit of the writing and worked with me on my messy first drafts helping me hone the material into this story. I am grateful for her expertise and her prayerfulness.

My brother Graeme Garrett, son Paul and daughter Karen gave generous time to reading the manuscript and offering many helpful insights for improving it. I value their loving support greatly. My friends, the holy scribblers – Irene Alexander, Christopher Brown, Charles Ringma, Terry Gatfield, John Steward and Neville Carr welcomed me into their group. Our writing retreats encouraged me in numerous practical ways with a shared rhythm of daily prayer, writing, readings of our work, laughter and discerning comments which have been invaluable.

To other friends who have given me unfailing practical and prayerful support in ways too numerous to enumerate here – Val and Keith Butler and Margaret Knight – my warmest thanks. And to Eugene Veith, the ordinary bloke who first invited me to listen to his story and so launched me on this journey – thank you for sharing your life with me and so many others.

www.ingramcontent.com/pod-product-compliance
Lightning Source LLC
Chambersburg PA
CBHW051428090426
42737CB00014B/2872